Reviewer Acclaim for Frank Swiderski, Window Snyder, and *Threat Modeling*

"This book shares a solid, practical approach to threat modeling and risk mitigation. The same process and tools have proven extremely efficient in developing secure, next-generation software at Microsoft."

Andres De Vivanco (security software engineer, Microsoft Security Business and Technology Unit)

"Threat modeling is the vital first step in constructing and deploying any software or system. Swiderski's and Snyder's book should be required reading for every software engineer."

Jonathan Pincus (architect, Programmer's Productivity Research Center, Microsoft Research)

Threat Modeling

Frank Swiderski
and Window Snyder

PUBLISHED BY
Microsoft Press
A Division of Microsoft Corporation
One Microsoft Way
Redmond, Washington 98052-6399

Library of Congress Cataloging-in-Publication Data
Swiderski, Frank.
    Threat Modeling / Frank Swiderski and Window Snyder.
       p. cm.
    Includes index.
    ISBN 0-7356-1991-3
    1. Computer security.   2. Computer networks--Security measures.   I. Snyder, Window.
   II. Title.

    QA76.9.A25S934   2004
    005.8--dc22   2004049976

Printed and bound in the United States of America.

1 2 3 4 5 6 7 8 9   QWE   9 8 7 6 5 4

Distributed in Canada by H.B. Fenn and Company Ltd.

A CIP catalogue record for this book is available from the British Library.

Microsoft Press books are available through booksellers and distributors worldwide. For further information about international editions, contact your local Microsoft Corporation office or contact Microsoft Press International directly at fax (425) 936-7329. Visit our Web site at www.microsoft.com/learning/books/. Send comments to *mspinput@microsoft.com*.

Acquisitions Editor: Robin Van Steenburgh
Project Editor: Karen Szall
Indexer: Richard Shrout

Body Part No. X10-46134

Table of Contents

Part III   Using Threat Modeling Effectively

Introduction

The process of threat modeling is not new. In truth, the concept of threat modeling did not originate in any book. The threat modeling methodology presented here and elsewhere is a process that attackers, security researchers, and others tend to follow inadvertently and have followed for some time. This is the strength of the approach this book advocates: it models the thought processes of an adversary who is attempting to achieve a set of goals with respect to a defined system.

A system can be attacked only if it has *entry points*—that is, transition points between the system in question and other systems that data or commands traverse. Furthermore, an adversary will attack a system only if that system has one or more assets of value. Based on these two ideas, threat modeling seeks to enumerate the goals an adversary has when attacking a system, investigate those goals for mitigation, and remedy them. In doing so, development teams begin creating a security specification for a system.

The term *threat* denotes an adversary's goal. Other texts might use this term to describe the adversary himself. Or they might use the term to describe the capability of an adversary to attack a system. In this book, however, threats refer to goals, and the sum of all goals for a system is considered the system's *threat profile*. In addition, the term *vulnerability* denotes a set of conditions that must occur or be true for a threat to be realized. This fits quite well with using threat trees to investigate threats to a system.

> **More Info**   Chapter 2 presents a more thorough list of the key threat modeling terms used in this book.

The Threat Modeling Process

This book presents a process that is certainly more formalized than what most attackers adhere to. Attackers do not take the time to enumerate all system assets, nor do they collect all the background information this book recommends. At the same time, the process could be even more formal than described in this book. The goal of this book is to describe a thought process, or methodology, that can be applied to any development environment—from the most casual to the most rigorous.

This book does not prescribe the use of Unified Modeling Language (UML) or any other formalized modeling as part of its methodology for a couple of reasons:

■   Not all development environments are the same, and not all developers use or are familiar with UML. The same is true for other modeling techniques. Instead of limiting the methodology to specific technologies, this book presents a process that can be integrated into any environment.

■   This methodology is intended to be customized; however, development teams need to adhere to its principles. Could development teams rewrite the process using UML? Certainly. Teams could also express the process in terms of other standards. For example, in Chapter 4, even the preferred data flow model—data flow diagrams (DFDs)—is interchangeable with other techniques.

Who Should Read This Book?

A number of members of project development teams can benefit from the methodology presented in this book:

■   **Security process managers (SPMs)**   The most important audience for this book is comprised of the SPMs of a development project. An SPM has the responsibility of applying the threat modeling methodology to the development environment. In addition, the SPM must drive the application security life cycle, educating other team members about the security process.

■   **Program managers**   These managers must "own" individual threat model documents and efforts, ensuring that they are scheduled and completed effectively for the system to benefit from them.

■   **Architects and developers**   Solution architects and developers will use the information in this book to guide them through the process of developing and understanding threats to the system so that they can create secure systems.

■ **Software testers** Testers, who play an important role in threat modeling, provide a critical eye to analyzing the security of the system. Testers must verify or disprove the security of the system, and they participate in threat models, reviews, and penetration tests.

What Will Development Teams Gain from This Book?

This book is not intended to be a list of common threats and vulnerabilities. Rather, it describes the process of threat modeling so that development teams can apply what they have learned to creating more secure systems. Every development environment has unique properties and characteristics. Teams reading this book are encouraged to customize the threat modeling methodology to suit their particular environments.

After reading this book, members of the development team will be able to:

■ Understand the adversary's view of a system and how it differs from an architect's or developer's view

■ Describe the threat profile for a system by using the data flow approach

■ Find weaknesses in system architecture and implementation by using investigation techniques, such as threat trees and threat model–directed code reviews

■ Provide a more credible characterization of the security of a system that has been threat modeled

■ Use threat modeling to verify the security of and increase the resilience of software systems

Development team members who want to skim this book for an overview should look at Chapter 2, which describes the overall threat modeling process. Chapters 3 and 5 will also be valuable to those looking for shortcuts because they describe entry points, assets, and the threat profile. Chapter 4 describes bounding the threat model discussion. The rest of the chapters, which flesh out the threat modeling process, will be most important for a project's security process manager.

The Book's Samples

This book features three running examples of threat models. Each of these samples represents a fictitious system or application:

- **Fabrikam Phone 1.0 application**   The Fabrikam Phone 1.0 threat model is used to present the abstract concepts of threat modeling, without tying those concepts to a particular type of software. The Phone 1.0 application is a typical telephone with caller ID, answering-machine functionality, and the ability of users to call in remotely and retrieve messages or modify their account configuration. In addition, this application has local access control features that enable it to be deployed in a public area while restricting calling features by an access code.

- **Humongous Insurance Price Quote Website**   The Humongous Insurance Price Quote Website threat model shows the threat modeling process applied to a simple Web application. The Price Quote Website allows users to request an insurance quote and insurance agents to provide responses.

- **A. Datum Access Control API**   The A. Datum Access Control API threat model presents a threat model for a software library. This example shows how threat modeling can be accomplished for a component that is not standalone, such as a feature area in a larger system or a reusable component that is integrated into other systems. The Access Control API is a simple library that determines whether a given user has read or write access to a resource. Resources are organized into a tree and must be mapped by the integrating system to physical resources, such as file paths.

The book's appendixes present these threat models in their entirety. As concepts in the threat modeling process are discussed throughout the book, samples from each threat model are explained. In addition to these three samples, the chapters of the book feature the running example of an office building, which applies the ideas presented to a nonsoftware system.

Support

Every effort has been made to ensure the accuracy of this book. Microsoft Press provides corrections for books at *http://www.microsoft.com/learning/support/*.

If you have comments, questions, or ideas about this book, please send them to Microsoft Press using either of the following methods:

Postal Mail:

Microsoft Press
Attn: Editor, Threat Modeling
One Microsoft Way
Redmond, WA 98052-6399

E-mail:

msinput@microsoft.com

To connect directly to the Microsoft Press Knowledge Base and enter a query regarding a question or issue that you have, go to *http://support.microsoft.com.*

Part I
Application Security

1

Introduction to Application Security

Software security is not a new field. Yet creating secure applications remains an elusive goal. Although this is especially true when the software has gone through several versions and includes legacy code that has not been subject to the current security process, new software can have security holes, too.

Creating a secure system requires a security process that is integrated into the application development cycle. But security exists at both the architecture and the implementation level, and the security plan must cover both areas. In addition, the roles in application security must be understood so that the process can be applied effectively.

Before this book delves into the threat modeling process, this chapter will provide some background information regarding application security, including:

■ An explanation of the historical approach to application security—and its failings

■ The use of code reviews during security design and implementation

■ The reasons application security is critical to business

■ The stages of the application security life cycle—and how threat modeling fits into the process

■ The architecture and implementation issues of ensuring application security

■ The different roles involved in creating a secure application

Historical Perspective: Setting the Stage for Threat Modeling

In the past, people relied on network security to prevent attacks. If they installed a firewall, they thought the network was protected. However, to allow anyone past the firewall to use the infrastructure, ports have to be opened for communications to pass through. A firewall cannot recognize the difference between legitimate use of an application and an attempted attack. A firewall can only analyze traffic for consistency within the network protocol, which is what a firewall does when detecting malformed packets.

Application proxies, which often are part of firewalls, can provide additional protection by inspecting network traffic for a specific application type to identify malicious use. However, because application proxies are general solutions applied to customized applications, they are typically inadequate and can have negative performance implications. For example, the application itself might have problems that both a firewall and an application proxy cannot detect, such as a payload that is described correctly by the protocol but, when processed, could cause a buffer overrun or integer overflow. (For more on buffer overruns, see the "Buffer Overruns" sidebar.)

Even though application proxies have become more sophisticated, their ability to predict flaws and cope with yet-unknown defects in the application they are protecting is not guaranteed. For example, an attack that takes advantage of an architecture flaw or logic flaw in an application, especially one with custom business logic, is unlikely to be prevented by a firewall or proxy. The flaw exists at too high a level in the protocol stack or simply is not anticipated. Therefore, the traffic goes through the open ports, allowing the flaw to be exploited.

Besides not being able to catch a large number of security issues, firewalls and proxies do not really address the problem—a security vulnerability in the application. For example, a buffer overrun in a Web server is not solved by placing a proxy in front of the server, even if doing so prevents exploitation from the general Internet. At some point, that overrun was written into the code for the system. Therefore, the issue should have been addressed during the application's design and development. This has become obvious as computers have become ubiquitous and as networking computers together, particularly through the Internet, has paved the way for mass exploitation of vulnerabilities.

Buffer Overruns

The buffer overrun is one of the most common implementation vulnerabilities. A buffer overrun occurs when an application copies more data to a memory region than it has previously allocated. This causes data in contiguous memory to be overwritten. An attacker can use a buffer overrun if he controls the data being copied to the memory. This allows him to overwrite contiguous data with information under his control. In some cases, such as on the stack, the contiguous memory can have program control flow information. In other cases, it might simply have data that affects program state. In any event, the attacker can change this data, causing the application to behave in an unintended manner. This usually results in the attacker forcing the target application to run arbitrary machine code of his choosing.

For example, in 1988 one of the propagation vectors for the Morris Internet worm exploited a buffer overrun. It might seem that this problem should have been solved by now, considering that more than 15 years have gone by. However, buffer overflows still occur. And Internet worms are still written to exploit them. Preventing buffer overflows involves far more than teaching developers to avoid creating them—it involves understanding the adversary and his motivations.

Code Reviews During Design and Implementation

One common method of addressing security that has become prevalent is using code reviews. Because the code review process is part of most development environments, it is a logical place to start. But code reviews are also slow and tedious affairs that can lead to boredom and missed bugs. In addition, a code review for application vulnerabilities will miss issues. For example, a code review probably will not be able to identify whether the authentication mechanism is strong enough for the security requirements of the application.

Finding Vulnerabilities in Architecture

Even a thorough code review will not find architecture-level vulnerabilities. A couple of reasons for this exist. First, the focus is too narrow; a line-by-line review of source code can retain only a limited context at best. Second, a code review addresses security after the fact—after it has been written into the application code. To counteract this, the development team must recognize both the implementation and architectural patterns that emerge. For example, any session-based system can be prone to the following architectural-level errors:

- **Guessable session identifiers** For session identifiers to be secure, they should not be predictable. If the attacker can determine the algorithm for generating session identifiers by using a small sample of legitimate IDs, she might be able to guess what the next few IDs will be. Once another user logs on to the system, the attacker would be able to spoof the identity of the user by employing a guessed session ID. (A "spoofed" transmission appears to come from a trusted source instead of the actual source.)

- **Session identifier replay** Session identifiers are a common method for identifying a user in systems that do not maintain connections across multiple requests, such as the Web. Session identifiers replace the need to authenticate every request, acting as a token that uniquely identifies the user once he is authenticated. However, if an adversary can acquire a session ID—for example, by sniffing network traffic—she will be able to send a malicious request containing the acquired session ID, which would appear to come from the original user. ("Sniffing" involves eavesdropping on network traffic and analyzing the communications.)

- **Injection attacks** Some session-based systems are *connection oriented,* meaning that they maintain a connection through the underlying transport between requests. Such systems often rely on the transport to identify the remote user, rather than using session identifiers. However, some transports are susceptible to an attacker "injecting" data into the connection stream, allowing him to spoof requests as though they were part of the legitimate user's session.

If the security architect examining the application is familiar with these kinds of attacks, the attacks might be identified. But how does a team of developers and testers with less familiarity with common architecture security issues identify these issues? How can security architects learn to identify security threats they have not previously encountered? Currently, security architects rely on their experience to recognize architecture-level security issues in applications. Teams that are trying to understand the risk their applications face have broad guidelines to work with and use methodology that often centers around brainstorming for the analysis components.

The threat modeling process described in this book enables anyone trying to examine the security architecture of an application to work with a procedural approach to identify commonly known architecture and implementation flaws, and to identify new issues—including those specific to a particular application. Threat modeling makes the application security analysis process less reliant on intuition and allows the program to more systematically enable people with less experience in security analysis to evaluate their application's security strength.

Finding Vulnerabilities in Implementation

Code review is a time-intensive process. There are tools available that can identify some kinds of implementation errors. These tools are currently very limited, both in number and functionality. Most of these tools produce a lot of output, little of which is helpful. Although the tools can identify unsafe code constructions, they are not adept at identifying which instances of a construct will result in a vulnerability. Currently these tools also are not adept at finding security vulnerabilities that occur with different signatures.

For example, a tool can easily identify that code is using a string function that does not perform bounds checking. However, most tools are not good at identifying a similar buffer overflow that occurs because a function is looping through some section and copying to a fixed buffer with either user-specified or incorrect completion criteria. Both cause overflows, but currently buffer overflows of the latter sort must be identified by a human. Even if tools could identify these buffer overflows reliably, they would not necessarily be able to identify whether the construction creates a security vulnerability.

Another problem with using these tools is that when they produce thousands of warnings on these issues, it can be difficult for a project manager to decide which potential vulnerabilities are worth fixing. Some of these constructions might be legitimate implementations. Some might indicate poor coding practice but not security vulnerabilities. Some might actually be vulnerabilities. Often destabilizing the code base by trying to fix all errors is cause for concern.

Fixing all errors might also be impractical or infeasible if a huge number of constructions are identified on a code base that might have millions of lines of code. The risk of introducing regressions with unnecessary changes in the code base can exist, and a project manager has the difficult task of determining which regressions to fix. And often, when the output of the tool is predominantly noise, people will stop using it and miss the few serious bugs it found.

Threat modeling creates a process that allows a team to identify the highest risk components in an application. This allows the team to identify which sections of the application would be best served by a code review. Threat modeling also allows a team to decide which bugs reported by code analysis tools are most likely to result in vulnerabilities and enables the team to reduce the number of fixes required. This is especially relevant when a security consultant is performing the code review because such efforts are expensive. A team that performs threat modeling on its own application is better equipped to identify high-risk areas than an outside security team that examines the application for a few weeks. The threat model can also be used to drive the external consultants' code review and penetration testing, making them focus on the areas with the most critical security exposure. This efficiency helps maximize the investment in the outside resources.

> **Tip**   By identifying these high-risk areas internally through threat modeling, a project manager can better focus an external team on a code review or penetration test to maximize the investment.

Why Application Security Is Critical to Business

When creating software that is not intended to be used commercially, the priority often is to create some required functionality. The security requirements for such a project are often not considered. Freeware developers who give their free time to create an application others find useful have the luxury of developing a program that meets the needs they have identified. Although some freeware developers consider security a priority, they often have no real requirement to address security. However, businesses that create software for internal use or for the consumer market must address customer expectations (for products), their own business risk (for internally deployed custom applications), or both (if the company deploys its own software).

Customer Expectations

Security is an aspect of reliability that most customers expect and all customers want. Customers expect that a product they buy will not introduce vulnerability into their computing environment, that access control mechanisms will not be circumvented, and that the application will maintain the integrity of the data it manages. If security is a feature of the product, customers might have even higher expectations and requirements, including the following:

- Reliability of transactions

- Data integrity during transmissions

- The presence of auditing mechanisms—especially if this differentiates this product from similar products

Different types of software have different security requirements. Commercial products are often deployed under a variety of scenarios that the developer often cannot predict or control. Although all customers associate security with reliability, they might have different expectations about product security. They also might consider security a feature as well as an aspect of reliability. The software vendor must be perceived as producing a secure product to maintain its customer base. Too many security issues—in some cases, even just one security issue—can damage the vendor's reputation as well as impact sales of the product.

Noncommercial software products (those not sold for profit) are created for various reasons, such as providing an alternative to for-pay systems, filling a real or perceived need, or selling consulting services for support. Although security flaws in these systems are equally as dangerous as those in commercial products—especially when noncommercial products are deployed instead of commercial ones—the perceived severity might not be as great.

Internal Enterprise Applications

Internal applications are developed for use within an enterprise. Security might be less of a priority because potential attackers are limited to people with access to the internal network. But the larger the corporation, the greater the chance of attacks by insiders such as disgruntled employees or opportunists. This is why businesses grant only certain employees access to certain enterprise applications, such as a corporate payroll system. Although attacks to internal applications are often easier to trace, they can cause significant damage. Therefore, preventing such attacks altogether is the preference.

Business Cost of Vulnerabilities

Regardless of the application type, the system's security is critical for business. This is true for both the software vendor and the end user. Vendors with repeated critical security vulnerabilities are likely to see decreased revenue from sales and increased costs from dealing with vulnerability reports from customers and third-party developers. Likewise, corporations that deploy insecure systems will see increased costs in patching vulnerabilities. Or worse, they might be actively exploited, resulting in arbitrary financial damage. In either case, the damage to a company's reputation will cause the loss of customers to other companies perceived as more secure. In addition, the increased visibility of software security flaws in the media only compounds the issue.

The Application Security Life Cycle

Applications have both a development life cycle and a corresponding security life cycle. These should not be separate processes; instead, to be effective, the security life cycle should be well integrated into the development life cycle. The security life cycle follows:

1. Gathering requirements

2. Securing design

3. Threat modeling

4. Performing implementation-level analysis (code review)

5. Performing penetration tests

6. Securing deployment

7. Integrating feedback

As with most processes, these phases have a degree of overlap, and each feeds into the next phase. In addition, some phases might cause the development team to revisit an earlier phase. For example, penetration testing might reveal architecture flaws that require the design to be revisited. Figure 1-1 shows the phases in the application security life cycle. The dotted lines between phases show how discoveries at any phase can result in a need to revisit earlier phases.

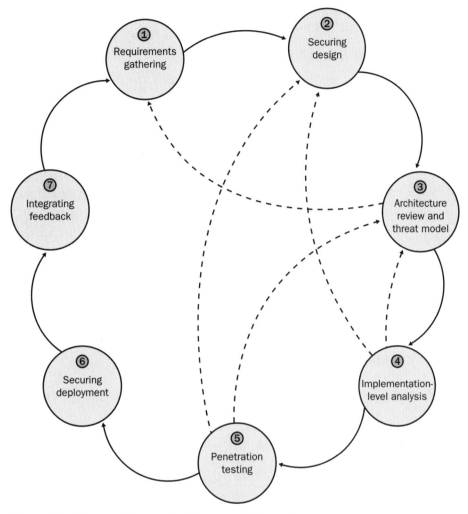

Figure 1-1   Phases in the application security life cycle.

Gathering Requirements

Requirements will differ depending on the kind of application being analyzed. For example, Web servers clearly have different requirements than text editors.

Considerations that might impact the application's security requirements include the following:

- Deployment environment
- Customer expectations
- Type of application
- Development team participants and their areas of expertise

Deployment Environment

If the application is being built for a specific deployment environment, as most internal corporate applications are, the requirements might not include flexibility. Because the application is intended to serve a single customer, having the flexibility to be deployed in alternate configurations is not a high priority. The single environment then drives design and implementation choices.

Developers of an application that might be deployed in many environments, such as a commercial product, have to consider flexible security options that will meet diverse customer needs. A product company cannot know how its product will actually be deployed, but it can make suggestions and let the customer know the assumptions the product makes about its environment.

Customer Expectations

When gathering requirements, developers must consider customer or end-user expectations. The development team should explore the following questions when gathering requirements for these applications:

- **Is this a security product?** Although customers will always expect products to be secure, security products have an even greater responsibility. An application that is deployed to protect a system or a network should not introduce new vulnerabilities into the environment. Security products are diverse and include firewalls, antivirus software, cryptographic libraries, intrusion detection systems, integrity maintenance and checking software, network scanners, and more. Customers rely on these tools to secure their entire computing environment. The integrity of these applications is paramount.

- **Is this application responsible for critical business infrastructure?** A customer expects reliability from the software that runs his business and cannot tolerate security vulnerabilities in these applications. These applications include mail servers and clients, Web servers, transaction servers, business productivity software, router firmware, telephony software, operating systems, databases, enterprise management software, and more. Patching these systems for security vulnerabilities is costly to a business. Customers need to minimize the downtime of these applications as much as possible. Because these are the applications that businesses must run for their day-to-day operations, they must tolerate their applications' security issues to keep their business running. It is the development team's responsibility to minimize the security risks of these application customers as much as possible.

■ **Is this application widely deployed? Does it use file types that are considered safe?**   Applications that are widely deployed have a significant impact on customers if a single vulnerability is found. For example, a security issue in a popular audio player can result in attackers manipulating seemingly harmless files, such as MP3s, into mechanisms for delivering an attack. If a vulnerability in an audio player allows a malformed MP3 to execute arbitrary code, an attacker might be able to propagate an attack easily on a file-sharing network. Examples of these at-risk applications include media players, Web browsers, file compression utilities, file readers, and imaging software.

Developers of any product that is widely deployed must consider the consequences of possible vulnerabilities on large audiences. Users deploying such applications trust that the files these applications display, play, or manipulate will not execute an attacker's instructions. This is true even when these files come from an untrusted location, such as the Internet.

■ **Is there external information that positions this product as more secure than its competitors?**   If the marketing language sets up these sorts of expectations, it goes without saying that the product had better deliver on these promises.

Type of Application

The nature of an application impacts its security requirements significantly. For example, Web servers and text editors have very different security requirements. An application that accepts connections from the network has a higher degree of risk than a stand-alone application. This does not imply that text editors have no risk, only that they have less risk. Thus, building a Web server requires a greater investment in security than building a text editor.

Applications that are accessible to untrusted users are at greater risk for security breaches than those that have restricted access. For example, mail servers typically accept network connections to receive mail from any user. This is the nature of Simple Mail Transfer Protocol (SMTP) and enables any user to send any other user e-mail over the Internet. A mail server has more risk than a virtual private network (VPN) server that also accepts connections from the Internet but allows little interaction before authentication. This nature of VPNs limits the bulk of the attack scenarios against such servers to authenticated users. Between authentication and auditing, it is easier to identify who is responsible for attacking applications such as VPN servers, which limits the risk a business faces for security vulnerabilities.

Applications that protect extremely valuable resources have higher security requirements than those protecting less valuable resources. Although this might seem obvious, do not overlook the implications. See the "Asset Value and Security" sidebar for details.

Asset Value and Security

Consider two embedded devices: a networked video game console and the software in a telephone switch. The video game console might accept connections from the Internet for multiplayer gaming, even from unauthenticated users. The worst-case security vulnerability scenarios for such an application include an attacker gaining control of the game console and potentially manipulating data stored in it, such as the high scores or credentials used to log in to gaming networks. The attacker might also use the console to launch attacks against other network users. These concerns vary from insignificant (the attacker changes or deletes the high scores) to significant (the attacker uses the console to establish a sniffer on the corporate network).

The software in a telephone switch presents a very different scenario. Compromising a switch could allow an attacker to redirect or monitor phone calls, disrupt services such as network and voice communication, and even prevent emergency services from getting messages. Even if the switch were on a limited network—which would reduce the risk to the software—the resources the switch protects might be so valuable that an attacker will work harder to find the vulnerabilities to gain access to and control them. Suffice it to say that a telephony switch requires more security consideration than a game console.

Who Develops the Security Requirements?

The customer, type of application, and type of assets to protect influence who should be involved in gathering requirements. The people involved in this phase of building commercial applications include the marketing, development, and test teams as well as the internal customers (if the commercial product is tested internally through deployment). Customer focus groups can also be used when relevant. Users of current software can provide invaluable information on the improvements they want to see in upcoming versions. For example, customers want fewer vulnerabilities; they want to patch less.

What kinds of security issues are of most concern to customers? For government and financial institutions, targeted attacks are a high priority. These institutions have highly valuable resources, meaning that people actively target them for attack. A successful compromise of such an environment can yield valuable data from or access to critical systems. The most sophisticated attackers have more to gain by attacking these systems than spreading chaos through worms and similar attacks.

In the business sector, worms, viruses, and widely launched attacks are a concern. Such Internet threats can cost businesses loss of revenue because of unforeseen downtime and loss of productivity.

Securing Design

Design must incorporate security considerations; security should never be an afterthought in the design process. If communications send sensitive data over a network, encrypt that data. If the application does a lot of data parsing, the parsing mechanism should be resistant to unexpected input. If an identifiable single point of failure exists, the system should be designed to withstand attacks to that component. Memory allocations should not be made based on data from user-specified sources.

These are the kinds of concerns the design team should address in the early design stages. Adding more functionality increases the attack surface of a system. Therefore, the design team must ask themselves if the feature is worth the security impact.

> **Important**   When choosing between design options, it is natural for developers to consider performance impact and which design scales best. Developers must also consider which designs are more secure and base their design choices on that information.

Threat Modeling

Threat modeling should be done when the project is feature complete. At this stage, the team can identify all entry points and feel confident that the attack surface will not change significantly before deployment. During threat modeling, the application is dissected into its functional components. The development team analyzes the components at every entry point and traces data flow through all functionality to identify security weaknesses.

Performing Implementation-Level Analysis (Code Review)

Implementation-level analysis, or code review, is most effective if the code is reviewed as features become code complete. Code review tools can help developers test their code before it is even checked into a build. Peer review is another efficient way to incorporate code review into the development schedule. A peer review can help reduce the number of implementation errors that are introduced with new code and revisions; plus, it also can be a great way to encourage accountability. No one wants to be the developer who introduced a buffer overflow that negatively impacts customers.

If performing code review on an existing code base that is too large to review line by line, use threat modeling to identify the components most at risk. Perform code review on these sections first, and then check the rest of the application over time as new versions are developed. Try to eliminate as much legacy code as possible. Eventually most (if not all) of the application will have had some level of implementation analysis for security vulnerabilities.

Unfortunately, new categories of vulnerabilities are found frequently. For example, format string vulnerabilities were not widely known or looked for until recently. The application must be reviewed for these new risks, as well. Incorporating code review into the development process is the best way to keep up with developments in the security world.

Performing Penetration Tests

Penetration testing should be incorporated into functional testing of an application. Threat modeling can help a test team develop methodical penetration testing plans.

> **More Info**   Penetration testing is discussed in Chapter 7. A complete guide to penetration testing network applications can be found in *Assessing Network Security* by Kevin Lam, David LeBlanc, and Ben Smith from the Microsoft Security Team (Microsoft Press, 2004).

Testing the application for security issues is critical. The development team must ask itself how well the application handles unexpected input.

Developers can create *fuzzers*—tools that test code by providing variations of malicious or malformed input—to generate data in the format the application is expecting but with modifications to test boundary conditions, unexpected data types, very long strings, negative numbers, and so on.

Developers should also ask themselves the following questions: Are there similar products on the market that have had security vulnerabilities? Could this product under development have similar issues? Are there known security issues in libraries or third-party code that this application has incorporated?

The development team should perform penetration testing as part of a security audit before the application is declared ready to ship. Vulnerabilities found during the audit should be fixed before the product ships.

Securing Deployment

Customers that deploy the application need to know the best practices for using the application in their environment and the assumptions made about the application's deployment environment. For example, if the product does send traffic between components on separate machines in the clear, this should be identified. In some deployments, this information might be considered sensitive. Therefore, administrators working on those deployments will need to know that they must include another protection for that transmission.

Some security features might not be enabled by default. During application development, the team sometimes makes these decisions as trade-offs with performance or usability. If the reasons for these decisions are not well documented, customers might not know they can take advantage of a particular security feature. Users often leave applications in their default configurations. Although the defaults should be as secure as possible, if an option not enabled by default exists, developers should make this clear in the product documentation.

Integrating Feedback

Once the application is in the hands of customers and users, issues will be identified, including security issues. If security issues are identified, make sure they are fixed either with security patches or in the next product version. Furthermore, the vulnerable components must be examined for similar issues. Any other applications using the offending technology must also be examined for vulnerability to the issue and similar issues.

A development team must have a plan in place for addressing possible vulnerabilities found by external parties. This prevents the scrambling that otherwise ensues when a critical issue is identified and customers are at risk.

Elements of Application Security

Two categories of application security errors exist: architecture and implementation. *Architecture issues* result from insecure design—for example, if the system has an authentication mechanism that cannot guarantee the identity of a remote user. *Implementation issues* result from insecure coding practices—for example, if the same system has a buffer overrun when an adversary sends an overly long username to the authentication component. The security of a system depends on both architecture and implementation.

> **Important**   Finding all the buffer overruns in a system that does not enforce the difference between an administrative user and a regular user does not make an application secure.

Threat modeling provides a methodical approach to analyzing application security that can be used to address both architecture and implementation issues. By understanding the adversary and the adversary's goals, a developer can design security into the application architecture. In addition, developers will understand the potential maliciousness of input and how secure coding practices can counter such attacks as overly long strings.

Architecture or Implementation Error?

The terms *architecture* and *implementation* are relatively straightforward. But when discussing security problems, classifying errors as architecture based or implementation based can be difficult. For example, earlier in the chapter, guessable session identifiers were labeled an architecture issue because a specification for a secure session management system should have guidelines on how IDs will be generated; for example, an ID might be generated by a cryptographically secure hash, rather than the less-secure C-library random function. An implementation error, on the other hand, would occur if the hash routine was written incorrectly.

(continued)

Architecture or Implementation Error?   *(continued)*

The challenge is determining where design stops and implementation begins. In some systems, the mechanism for session management might not be specified. Therefore, it could be argued that the developer's choice of using *rand()* to generate session identifiers is an implementation issue. For this book's purposes, however, architecture and implementation issues will be defined like this:

- An architecture issue can reasonably be remedied by secure design practices. The application's architects are responsible for such issues.

- An implementation issue is a problem that even the most junior developers would be expected to avoid, based on the team's secure-coding guidelines.

This distinction is important because, while threat modeling can be used to find both architecture and implementation issues, the latter is best found through code review and penetration tests that are directed by threat models. In either case, threat modeling a system early on can prevent issues by giving the development team the knowledge necessary to understand the system's threat profile and deal appropriately with malicious input.

Architecture

An application's architecture is its blueprints. Secure applications have specifications that outline the security needs of the system to counter threats. A system architect must understand the potential system threats to design a resilient system and determine which security features are necessary and relevant, and which are superfluous.

> **Important**   Every legitimate security feature counters one or more threats to the system. This basic premise is reason enough to perform threat modeling.

An authentication mechanism is an example of a critical component for a distributed application's security. This mechanism must have a specification associated with it to counter spoofing, elevation of privilege, and repudiation threats. Otherwise, the developer must create this specification. Although many developers are also architects or capable of architecting a secure system, creating this specification is still not an implementation task. Instead, implementing without a specification becomes an ad hoc design task, making it more prone to vulnerabilities.

Clearly, architecture plays a role in a system's security. Threat modeling can be used to both prevent and find issues in an application's design. When developers begin threat modeling at design time, threats are immediately recognized and countered by proactively specifying how a system should prevent them. If threat modeling is performed after the design has been created, it can uncover threats that have no mitigation in the system's design.

Implementation

Implementation is also critical to application security. Even a secure design is susceptible to security breaches if it is not implemented by using secure coding practices. Numerous references for these practices exist, and this book is not the right place to repeat them. However, threat modeling does play an important part in creating secure implementation.

Threat modeling takes a data flow approach to application security. It helps the team understand where input comes from and how an adversary can manipulate it to cause the system to fail. Recognizing that data could be tainted can impact implementation. The driving factor here is that the developer cannot make assumptions about the characteristics of input. For example, a path name supplied to a function should not be assumed to be shorter than the system-defined maximum path length. Or an integer should not be assumed to be within a certain range. Many such examples exist, but the important point is realizing that data is unlikely to correspond to a specification if that data originates from an adversary.

> **More Info**   For more information about implementation-level security, an excellent source is *Writing Secure Code, Second Edition*, by Michael Howard and David LeBlanc (Microsoft Press, 2003).

Integer Overflows

An integer overflow (and in some cases, underflow) results when the application developer neglects to check for rollover in an arithmetic operation. On a 32-bit processor, the largest native unsigned integer is 4,294,967,295, with the smallest being, of course, zero (0). If an addition is performed and the result is greater than the extent of the range for the integer, the value wraps. So, adding 1 to 4,294,967,295 gives the result of 0. Subtracting 1 from 0 will result in 4,294,967,295. Any operation that results in the integer's minimum or maximum value being crossed is an *integer overflow*. Complicating this is the fact that integer overflows work differently for signed integers. A 32-bit signed integer wraps at the values 2,147,483,647 and –2,147,483,648. Other types of integers, such as unsigned short integers, have different extents, for example, 0 to 65,535.

Integer overflows are problematic because they are exploitable in multiple ways and their detection is difficult. One exploit method, using signed integers, could allow a hacker to use negative indices in an array, allowing him to address elements before the first element. Because this area of memory is not actually part of the array and is probably used for some other data, the effects of a read or write operation here could be disastrous. Another exploit method uses an integer overflow to cause a buffer overflow. Strings are usually null-terminated—that is, there is a single 0 character at the end of the string to denote its end. Consider a case where a string length is stored in an unsigned short integer and the length is 65,535 characters. The code that allocates memory for the string will typically add one character for the null termination. The result is an allocation of zero characters. However, when the string is copied and the original length is used, 65,535 characters are copied to a space that can hold zero characters.

There are other scenarios where integer overflows result in exploitable conditions. The problem is, first, that they are often use-specific, that is, the exploit vector depends on how the integer is being used. And second, integer overflows are difficult to detect in an automated fashion because the noise level of legitimate arithmetic operations is high.

Roles in Application Security

Roles must be defined to drive the security process. The most important role to define is that of security process manager—the person who will own the application security life cycle, the threat modeling process, and how this process fits into the development life cycle. Although security is the entire team's job, one person needs to coordinate the security efforts and be accountable.

In addition to the role of security process manager, each person on the development team fills a specific role:

- Architects are primarily responsible for designing secure systems. Architects must play a role in threat modeling because they design solutions based on functional requirements. Because this design is the foundation of the system, the involvement of architects in the security process is critical.

- Developers create the system based on the design and must not introduce new vulnerabilities into either architecture or implementation. Because developers straddle both areas, their involvement in the security process is critical. Developers have the most intimate knowledge of the technical aspects of the system and should be both a primary source and consumer of information in the threat modeling process. Developers also perform security code reviews for their peers.

- Testers need to find existing vulnerabilities and create test plans that address every threat scenario identified in the threat modeling process. Testers must question both architecture and implementation, rather than just testing to functional requirements. They also need to be conscious of vulnerabilities in similar products and determine whether their product is vulnerable to the same issues. Testers are often responsible for performing security penetration testing of a product.

- Managers make choices about how much security work is relevant for their product. They answer such questions as: How much time and money can the company spend? How is the team's time best used? Managers must demonstrate return on investment (ROI) for all security work, and they must justify feature changes or the time it takes to fix a bug once identified.

Summary

Application security is not new, and exploitation of security issues continues to occur. This has given rise to an industry of software vendors and security consultancies, all vying to address these problems. Although security processes are not new, many services offered in the security industry continue to start from scratch or offer partial solutions to a much larger problem.

Threat modeling has origins in previous standards of security analysis. Although the process outlined in this book is unique in its presentation of a way of thinking about security, it is grounded in processes that have existed for several decades.

Clearly, the security of an application can affect a corporation's bottom line. Rehashing the importance of security can seem monotonous, but vendors continue to create insecure systems. This must be countered by integrating the application security life cycle, including threat modeling, into the development life cycle by addressing both architecture- and implementation-level security threats.

To integrate security as a process, development teams must assign ownership and roles in the security life cycle. Without ownership, no accountability exists, making it easy to point fingers at someone else when a vulnerability is publicly discovered. Ownership helps drive security processes so that the quality of applications can be improved.

2

Why Threat Modeling?

Threat modeling is a method of assessing and documenting the security risks associated with an application. This methodology can help development teams identify both the security strengths and weaknesses of the system and can serve as a basis for investigating potential threats and testing and investigating vulnerabilities.

The threat modeling process involves understanding an adversary's goals in attacking a system based on the system's assets of interest. This is critical to producing a secure system because threats are the justification for security features at both the architectural and implementation level.

Threat modeling answers the need for a methodical thought process in analyzing the security of a system. Although this book lists specific data points to be collected during the threat modeling process, its primary focus is the methodology for creating attack goals that can be used to secure a system. Each organization should customize this process to its programming environment.

This chapter covers the following topics:

- Defining the threat modeling process and outlining its purpose, objectives, and high-level steps

- Explaining this book's approach to threat modeling—from understanding one's adversaries to incorporating threat modeling into the application life cycle

- Describing how to organize a threat model

> **Note**   Threat modeling builds on many existing security analysis tools and techniques. Although some of its credibility is borrowed from these existing processes, threat modeling has been gaining popularity at Microsoft and other organizations. The results of threat modeling are evident in architecture bugs being found earlier or avoided completely as well as implementation that takes into account the adversary and has fewer vulnerabilities upon thorough code review.

Defining Threat Modeling

Threat modeling looks at a system from an adversary's perspective to anticipate attack goals. Threat modeling is based on the premise that an adversary cannot attack a system without a method of supplying it with data or otherwise interacting with it. Furthermore, the adversary will not attack the system without assets of interest.

Threat modeling looks at a system's *entry points* (in other words, interfaces the system has with the outside world) to determine the functionality that an adversary can exercise on the system and what assets he can affect. This allows development teams to enumerate attack goals, or *threats*. *Vulnerabilities* are discovered when a threat is investigated and safeguards are proven insufficient, or when no mitigation of the threat is in place.

Threat modeling produces a threat model document. This document contains the data points collected in the steps discussed in Chapters 3 through 5 and should be considered a living document. That is, as the software that was modeled changes, the document should be updated to reflect this. It is important to remember that the document contains sensitive information about the system and, therefore, it should be appropriately protected and tracked. Threat model documents are used as a basis for security specifications and security testing and can also be used to gauge the effectiveness of the threat modeling process. Since they document what was accomplished during threat modeling, these documents can help prevent duplication of effort later on.

> **Note**   Other sources on threat modeling might refer to threats as *entities,* such as a perpetrator or an adversary. In this book, however, the term *threat* denotes an adversary's attack goal for a specific system.

Threat Modeling Terminology

Before discussing the threat modeling process, certain terms should be defined. These will be explored in more detail in subsequent chapters:

- **Asset**   An abstract or concrete resource that a system must protect from misuse by an adversary.

- **Attack path**   A sequence of conditions in a threat tree that must be met for an attack goal (threat) to be achieved. A valid attack path (one with no mitigated conditions) is a vulnerability.

- **Condition**   A single action or weakness that must be present in an attack path for a threat to be unmitigated and therefore exploitable as a vulnerability.

- **DREAD**   A ranking of the risk associated with a condition or vulnerability: Damage potential, Reproducibility, Exploitability, Affected users, and Discoverability.

- **Entry point**   An interface that the system has with the outside world—that is, the transition point between some functionality controlled by the system and that which is outside its control.

- **External dependency**   A dependency on another system that the security of the system being modeled must abide by to prevent potential vulnerabilities.

- **External entity**   A system, user, or other component that exists outside the system being modeled but can interact with that system via one or more entry points.

- **Penetration test**   A test of the implementation of a system that attempts various attack paths, to either prove or disprove the mitigation of one or more threats.

- **Risk**   A characterization of the danger of a vulnerability or condition.

- **Security strength**   The effectiveness of the system at mitigating a threat.

- **Security weakness**   An insufficient mitigation of a threat to the system, usually resulting in a vulnerability.

- **STRIDE**   A classification system that describes the effect of a threat: Spoofing, Tampering, Repudiation, Denial of service, and Elevation of privilege—in other words, what an adversary will attain if the threat is exploited as a vulnerability.

- **System**   A collection of functionality that can span one or more components (functional areas). A system exposes certain functionality to external entities (interactors outside of the control of the system) and must protect one or more assets.

- **Threat**   The adversary's goals, or what an adversary might try to do to a system. (The collection of all threats against a system is its threat profile.) Threats to a system always exist, regardless of mitigation.

- **Threat model**   A document that provides background information on a system, the system's threat profile, and an analysis of the current system against that threat profile.

- **Threat profile**   A characterization of all attack goals that an adversary has for a system. A threat profile explains what the adversary might try to do with or to the system's assets. Simply put, it is a list of threats.

- **Threat tree**   An analysis tool that describes the attack paths for a particular threat. A threat tree is comprised of hierarchical conditions and allows the threat's mitigation (or lack thereof) to be characterized. The root of the threat tree is the threat that it corresponds to.

- **Trust level**   A characterization of an external entity, often based on how it is authenticated and what privileges it has. Trust levels can be associated with entry points. In this case, the trust level would describe the minimum trust that an external entity should have to interface with the entry point. Trust levels can also be associated with protected resources, in which case a trust level would describe the minimum trust that an external entity should have to influence the resource.

- **Use scenario**   How the system is intended (or not intended) to be used.

- **Vulnerability**   A security flaw in the system that represents a valid way for an adversary to realize a threat. A threat that has an unmitigated attack path from the path's leaf conditions in a threat tree to the root threat results in a vulnerability.

Purpose and Objectives

Threat modeling is, in essence, the act of creating a security design specification and later testing that design. Thus, threat modeling is integral to the development of any secure system. If performed thoroughly and to a standard methodology, threat modeling can improve the built-in security of a system as well as user confidence in that security. To accomplish this heightened security, threat modeling strives to

■ **Understand the threat profile of a system.**   The threat profile is an enumeration of all the adversary's goals for the system, regardless of whether they are known to be mitigated. Note that the threat profile is not an enumeration of the *attack vectors,* which are specific methods of exploiting a vulnerability.

■ **Provide a basis for secure design and implementation.**   Based on the threat profile of the system, the development team can justify security features or prescribe secure implementation practices. Put simply, one cannot implement a secure system without understanding what she is securing it against.

■ **Discover vulnerabilities.**   Using techniques such as threat trees to analyze attack vectors, threat modeling can find architectural vulnerabilities as well as direct code reviews and penetration tests to find implementation vulnerabilities.

■ **Provide feedback for the application security life cycle.**   Threat modeling is used to verify the security of the system at design time. It provides a framework for penetration testing and can direct code reviews to high-risk components of the system.

Analyzing the security of an application does not simply involve finding security bugs. The information produced during threat modeling is used for multiple purposes. As stated previously, one goal of a threat model is to thoroughly characterize the threat profile of a system. In other words, given the purpose and functionality of a system, a threat model describes all the possible goals that an adversary has for that system. This characterization is agnostic to whether these threats are actually vulnerabilities.

Although this sounds like an extensive amount of work (and that simply looking for vulnerabilities would be easier), such an approach would not only be incomplete, it would fail to characterize the *security strengths* of a system. This is often difficult to quantify: How secure is the system? If a threat model fully describes the system's threat profile, that question is answered by determining the level of mitigation against each threat, weighted against the threat's associated risk.

Another important aspect of threat modeling is determining the *security weaknesses* of the system. One can analyze the unmitigated threats to determine where an adversary might try to attack the system and what he might attain if the attack were successful. Because threat modeling takes into account all types of attacks against the system, it can identify not only implementation improvements, but also areas where a design change could improve security across the board.

Threat modeling also feeds directly into security testing. The logical analysis of threats characterizes how an adversary might try to attack the system and breaks down such an attack into monatomic conditions. These conditions typically present testable scenarios, rather than vaguer high-level threats. In addition, threat modeling often identifies areas that are best analyzed during a focused security push or penetration test, making such a push better organized and more effective.

Examining the Threat Modeling Process

Threat modeling is comprised of three high-level steps: understanding the adversary's view, characterizing the security of the system, and determining threats. Each of these steps has logical substeps. However, threat modeling is not strictly linear. For example, additions are often made to the background information, such as what dependencies the system has on other systems or what scenarios are outside the scope of the threat model, when threats are identified as a result of the system being better understood. The strength of the threat modeling process lies primarily in the information and analysis concepts. Figure 2-1 offers an overview of the threat modeling process.

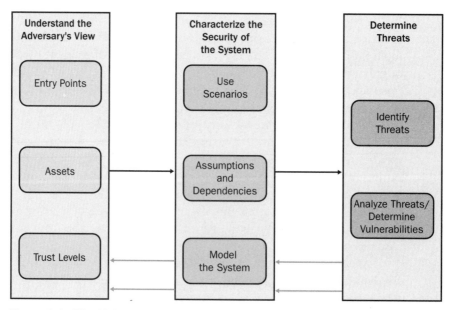

Figure 2-1   The high-level process of threat modeling.

Understanding the Adversary's View

Understanding the adversary's view of the system is a critical first step in the threat modeling process. Threat modeling takes an outside-in approach because such an approach most closely models the adversary's view. Therefore, understanding the adversary's view entails enumerating entry points and assets, as well as cross-referencing them with trust levels. Chapter 3 covers each of these topics in more detail.

Entry Points

Entry points are any location where data or control transfers between the system being modeled and another system. To identify a system's entry points, one must ask how an adversary can interface with the component. Entry points show all the places where the adversary can attack the system, including transfer points such as open sockets, remote procedure call (RPC) interfaces, Web services interfaces, and data being read from the file system. Entry points should be listed regardless of the privilege level required to interface with them. Note, however, that this information is still captured in the form of cross-referenced trust levels.

Assets

Assets are the resources the component or system has that an adversary might try to modify, steal, or otherwise access or manipulate. Assets can be tangible, such as a process token, or more abstract, such as data consistency (for example, a string class that maintains a length field). Assets are the basis for threats. It is impossible to have a threat without a corresponding asset because assets are essentially threat targets. As with entry points, the trust levels of assets are cross-referenced.

Trust Levels

Trust levels define how external entities are characterized for the system. Trust levels are often broken down according to privileges assigned or credentials supplied, and they are used to prioritize discussion in threat modeling meetings. In addition, they are cross-referenced with entry points and protected resources. Trust levels define the privilege that an external entity should have to legitimately use an entry point or functionality at the entry point, and they dictate which assets external entities should normally be allowed to access or affect in some way.

Characterizing the Security of the System

Characterizing the security of the system involves bounding the threat model, gathering information about dependencies that are critical to security, and understanding the internal workings of the system. This characterization provides the necessary information for people to understand the threat model. Modeling the system helps the team identify design-specific and implementation-specific threats. To characterize a system's security level, one must

1. Define use scenarios.

    Development teams must ask themselves how the component or system will be used. Conversely, the teams can ask themselves how the component or system will *not* be used. Use scenarios bound the threat modeling discussion, pointing out situations beyond the security architecture. Use scenarios can also be used as mitigation later in the process.

2. Identify assumptions and dependencies.

    Development teams should collect information such as external dependencies, external and internal security notes, and implementation assumptions. External dependencies document contingencies on other systems that affect the security of the system being modeled. External and internal security notes provide information to the system user and the person reading the threat model, respectively, which is critical to understanding the security of the system. Implementation assumptions provide security information to the developer that is critical to applying parts of the system in a secure manner.

3. Model the system.

    Data flow diagrams (DFDs) or other diagrams, such as process models, are used to understand the actions a system performs at a given entry point. DFDs are visual representations of how a system processes data. These diagrams answer questions such as: How are protected resources affected? Where could an external entity manipulate an asset? What processing occurs beyond an entry point? What action is taken on behalf of the external entity, or what transformation is performed on the data supplied? These answers help development teams understand what an adversary might do at a given entry point.

Determining Threats

Enumerating threats creates a threat profile for a system, describing all the potential attacks that architects and developers should mitigate against. As discussed earlier, threats with valid attack paths are considered vulnerabilities. The security of a system can be expressed in terms of threats with appropriate mitigation vs. total threats, taking into account the severity of the threats with insufficient mitigation. To create a threat profile for a system, development teams must

1. Identify threats.

    For each entry point, the development team determines how an adversary might try to affect an asset. Based on what the asset is, the team predicts what the adversary would try to do and what his goals would be—this is where the STRIDE classification system comes into play. (Chapter 5 provides more information about the STRIDE classifications.)

2. Analyze threats.

    Development teams model threats to determine whether they are mitigated. Using threat trees, a development team can decompose a threat into individual, testable conditions. Threats that are not mitigated become vulnerabilities—security bugs that must be remedied.

How Threat Modeling Fits into the Application Security Life Cycle

Threat modeling should be an integral process in the application security life cycle. Not only does threat modeling provide a basis for assessing the security architecture of the system, it also can be used as a penetration test plan and a tool to direct security code reviews. Ideally, threat modeling starts when the architects design the system. The threat model document is updated during development phases, when the architecture is done, and when code is complete. Figure 2-2 shows how the various players in application development contribute to the threat modeling process.

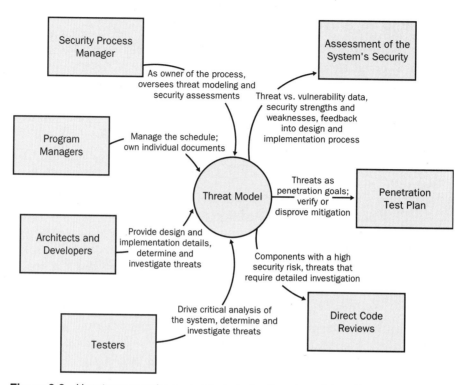

Figure 2-2   How team members contribute to the threat model and how threat models can be used in the application security life cycle.

This section explains the three primary outputs of threat modeling into the application security life cycle: assigning the system's security, planning for penetration testing, and driving code reviews.

Assessing the System's Security

One goal of threat modeling is to understand the threat profile of the system. Again, the threat profile is a complete list of the security threats that are always present for the system. Analyzing these threats allows the team to understand how well the system is protected, which in turn shows the system's security strengths and weaknesses.

Aside from moving toward quantifiable security, threat models provide a qualitative analysis of system security. The more vulnerabilities found in a threat model, the weaker the system. This can cause architects and developers to revisit a system design or particular implementation.

The Realities of Quantifying Security

Although it is impossible to assign a quantifiable security rating to a system, threat modeling provides a basis for characterizing relative security. First, it provides the ratio of unmitigated threats to total threats, which yields a general security rating, assuming that the threat profile is complete. If several versions of a system have gone through the threat modeling process, a relative number can be more informative. For example, version n might have a 5 percent unmitigated ratio, whereas version $n+1$ might have a 3 percent ratio. In theory, this shows that the security of the system is increasing. In practice, however, this comparison is flawed. This is because the more recent system version likely will have new features that increase the threat profile of the system, making a direct comparison of mitigation rates approximate at best. In addition, the results must be weighed with risk. For instance, the 5 percent ratio might represent low-risk issues, while the 3 percent ratio might represent high risks.

Planning for Penetration Testing

A threat model is inherently a plan for penetration testing. *Penetration testing* is the process of attacking a system to achieve specific goals corresponding directly to the threats in the threat model. (If attack goals exist in a penetration test that are not included in the threat profile, the threat profile is obviously incomplete.) Whereas threat models investigate threats through architectural review, threat trees, and the like, penetration testing investigates threats by directly attacking a running system.

Penetration tests can be *informed* or *uninformed*. An informed penetration test gives testers knowledge of the internals of the system that they can use to help attack the system. Uninformed testing, or black box testing, does not reveal this information and more closely simulates an adversary attacking a closed-source system. The advantage of the informed penetration test is that testers spend less time trying to understand the system and more time actually attacking it. On the other hand, with informed tests, findings might be based on having insider knowledge that an adversary or black box tester would not have. Therefore, uninformed testing provides an opportunity to see how much an adversary could discover without this insider knowledge.

The threat profile can be used to drive the penetration test. Testers attempt to prove or disprove threat mitigation. In addition, testers might find threats that are not covered by the threat model, causing them to revisit the threat model.

Penetration testing is one method of verifying the work done during threat modeling or, in some cases, a method for investigating threats.

Driving Code Reviews

Threat modeling will identify high-risk areas of the system that receive the majority of threats. These areas are often good candidates for directed code reviews and typically include components such as protocol parsers, access control components, and session management mechanisms. High-risk areas typically interface directly with an external entity or deal with data in flexible formats.

Line-by-line code reviews of these high-risk areas are important because an area with a large number of threats typically has complicated security requirements. Therefore, analyzing the code for design inconsistencies or insecure coding practices can yield subtle vulnerabilities that otherwise would be missed.

Some threats identified during threat modeling are best investigated through code reviews. This is often the case when the threat targets less familiar legacy code, where the original developers have retired or long since moved to other positions. This is also the case when the threat is far-reaching and the team must look to the code to understand the threat implications. Finally, threats that deal with potential implementation issues (for example, handling malformed input) are best investigated with a review of the associated code.

Organizing a Threat Model

To schedule, organize, and write a successful threat model, keep in mind the following suggestions:

- **Start threat models early.**   Much of the background information collected during the creation of a threat model is best documented when the specification is being written. For example, entry points, trust levels, protected resources, and use scenarios are usually known at design time (though they might be refined when implementation occurs).

- **Consider a weekly threat model meeting.**   During the meeting, feature teams can take advantage of having a consistent security group to help with their threat model. The regular participants can use their exposure to feature-level threat models to create application-level threat models. This also helps prevent putting off the writing of threat models until the last minute.

- **Include people with security experience that are not familiar with the system.**   Including someone who has not worked on the system can negate any unintentional bias about its functionality that stems from having designed or developed the system.

- **Start with a meeting to discuss the functionality of the system being modeled.**   Reviewing the purpose and features of the system provides a clear understanding of what is being modeled. This also helps to bound the threat model discussion to a clearly defined area.

- **Document off line.**   Filling out the entire threat model document during threat model meetings would be inefficient.

- **Take notes in the document, but add more specific details after the meeting.**   In addition, some parts of the document should be filled out before such meetings.

- **Focus on threats rather than mitigation.**   Once threats have been enumerated, determine whether there is sufficient mitigation on all attack paths. Discussing mitigation during a threat enumeration session can drag out the threat model meeting.

- **Remember the audience for the threat model.**   By reading the document, managers should be able to assess the security of the product. Testers should be able to take the document and construct security tests. Security review teams should be confident that all threats were considered when the component was designed and implemented.

Summary

Threat modeling is a methodology for analyzing security in a system. Used effectively, threat modeling can find security strengths and weaknesses, discover vulnerabilities, and provide feedback into the security life cycle of the application. Threat modeling consists of understanding the adversary's view of the system, characterizing its security, and determining and investigating threats.

This book will explain the concepts behind threat modeling and how it can benefit the security of any system. Readers should customize the threat modeling process detailed in this book for their own development environments. The key threat modeling concepts covered in the book, however, are based on years of security research and proven methodologies.

Part II
Understanding Threat Modeling

3

How an Adversary Sees
an Application

As described in Chapter 2, threat modeling involves the process of determining an adversary's goals for a given application or system. Figuring out an adversary's goals requires understanding how an adversary sees the application. The adversary's view is not the same as that of the application developer or architect. An adversary is driven by the desire to acquire access to the application's assets.

Two constraints prevent an adversary from compromising an application: the finite set of entry points into the application and the level of trust that the application grants to a person using the entry point. Unless adversaries have access to design specifications or source code, they view the application as a black box. Even if adversaries have specifications and source code (which reveal the inner workings of the application), their perspective when attacking the application is still from the outside in and is governed by the services exposed (intended or unintended).

Contrast this with the view of the application's architect and developer, whose perspective is inside out. Architects and developers design and build an application by planning and writing components and features that ultimately provide a service to the user. The development team must create threat models to understand the security architecture of the application it is building. In addition, the team must try to mimic the adversary's view to determine his goals.

This chapter covers the following topics:

- Identifying the adversary's goals in attacking the application

- Understanding the principles of the data flow approach

- Analyzing entry points
- Determining the assets of interest to the adversary
- Working with trust levels

The Adversary's Goals

Identifying the intentions of an adversary involves a combination of application-specific analysis and awareness of the goals for the platform, language, and services that the application uses or provides. These goals are considered threats, and they are a primary output of the threat modeling process.

To determine an adversary's goals, a thorough threat model must take the view of the adversary and avoid making assumptions or drawing conclusions. This critical analysis is particularly important for the application's architects and developers.

> **Important**   An application should be considered unsafe until demonstrated to be otherwise.

A good threat model cannot be created by simply brainstorming an adversary's possible intentions. Although participants in a brainstorming session sometimes find serious flaws in an application, they often do so only because they already have experience in analyzing application security. More important, this approach does not provide the complete analysis warranted to characterize an application's security, and ideally, to demonstrate that it is safe.

Creating a good threat model requires a more systematic approach. Threats must be determined not by revelations or luck, but by understanding the application's entry points, assets of interest, and requisite trust levels. These are the elements an adversary will be targeting; the members of the threat modeling team must understand these elements and their implications to create an effective threat model.

How does the threat modeling team know when it has analyzed all the necessary areas of the application for strengths and weaknesses? What are the metrics for determining when the threat model is finished? Brainstorming will uncover some ideas, but inevitably some threat will be missed using this unstructured approach. However, by using a process-based methodology, such as the *data flow approach* presented in the next section, teams can ensure that they analyze every entry point, at every level of access, for every use case, and targeting every asset. Once teams have done this, they can be confident that the threat model is complete—and that the security architecture of the application is well understood.

Principles of the Data Flow Approach

The data flow approach to threat modeling follows the adversary's data and commands as they are processed by the system, analyzing how they are parsed and acted on, as well as noting which assets they interact with. Because an adversary can attack only the parts of the application that she can exercise in this manner, the data flow approach shows where the application could be susceptible to security failures. Data flow diagrams (DFDs), discussed in Chapter 4, are used to pictorially represent these threat paths (the sequence of processing that occurs on the adversary's data or commands).

The data flow approach also provides a systematic approach to threat modeling. Rather than simply brainstorming threats, the threat modeling team follows data and commands through the system from the entry points. Any transformation or action on behalf of the data could be susceptible to threats. Thus, the team is better able to enumerate threats because at any point they are dealing with a specific processing action on specific data from a specific entry point.

The data flow approach is based on the following principles:

- **An application cannot be attacked unless the adversary has a way to interact with it.**   In most cases, the adversary must actively jeopardize the application's security, either by directly invoking some functionality or by supplying the application with data through various means. Examples of the latter include editing a configuration file that is processed by the application or, in the case where the threat model is for a feature area, supplying data to another component in the application which eventually passes the data to the feature in question. The remaining passive attacks (those attacks where the adversary simply consumes data from the application) are information disclosure attacks. In this case, the adversary is still interacting with the application by listening on the appropriate channel, which might be a network, an event, or another message channel. For example, some wireless applications broadcast information that is unsolicited. A passive attacker who listens for this information could discover valuable information about the application.

■   **An asset of interest to the adversary must exist.** This second principle is just as important as the first. An adversary's goals are always based on the system's assets. The adversary has no reason to attack the system unless it contains something of value to her—for example, corporate or personal data, processing resources, or financial information.

Analyzing Entry Points

Entry points are where control or data crosses the boundary of the system being modeled. Suppose that the system is an office building. The doors to the building are obvious entry points because they allow people and items to enter and leave the building. If the system being modeled is constrained to the building, everything outdoors is considered external. Because the doors allow objects to move (or flow) between the system and the external world, they are entry points. Figure 3-1 shows the entry points in a typical office building.

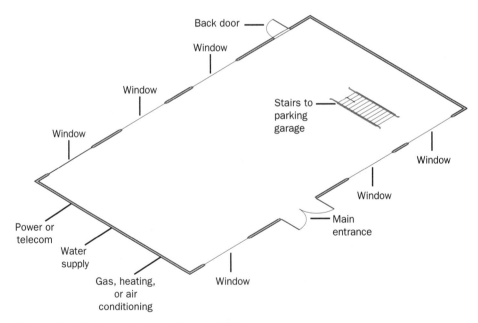

Figure 3-1 Entry points of an office building.

To the adversary, entry points represent a means of interacting with the system and are therefore considered *attack points*. In the office building example, if an adversary wants to gain access to the building, perhaps to conduct industrial espionage, the doors leading to the outside would be an obvious way to gain access.

Entry points include all junctions between the system and external components. Consider the office building again. The doors leading outside are not the only entry points. The building's windows are also obvious entry points. But what about other junction points comprising the building's infrastructure, such as the water pipes, telecommunication and data connections, electrical wiring, and air conditioning ducts? Interaction with the outside world occurs though all these points.

Infrastructure Entry Points

Unlike clear entry points, such as an office building's doors and windows, infrastructure entry points are sometimes overlooked by application development teams. *Infrastructure entry points* can include data that is read from the file system or configuration store, such as a registry. When threat modeling an application, architects and developers must consider all entry points that represent a transition of control or data to or from the application. These include points of interactions with other applications, network data such as Domain Name Service (DNS) responses and network time services, APIs, and administrative controls.

Exit Points

Exit points share similar characteristics with entry points and should therefore be included in any threat model analysis of application entry points. As with entry points, exit points represent locations where control or data moves between the system and the external world. In the office building example, a garbage dumpster behind the building is one such junction with the external world, and one where data can be disclosed without an external entity actively soliciting it. If an attacker were to rummage through a dumpster, he could uncover a sizable amount of company information. Some unscrupulous individuals frequently engage in such "dumpster diving" to collect sensitive information about people and corporations.

> **Tip**   Although exit points rarely pose a threat beyond information disclosure, the data an adversary can acquire at an exit point might result in other types of attacks. Thus, it's safest to include exit points in the entry point enumeration of a threat model.

Layered Entry Points

Entry points in a system can be layered, such as in a Web application, as Figure 3-2 illustrates. Each Web page can be considered an entry point because a potential adversary can use a request for a particular page to interact with the application. But many Web pages serve multiple yet disparate functions based on the information in a particular request. For example, imagine a website that serves a Web page called MyAccount.asp. That page may perform different actions based on the *Action* parameter. A request for */MyAccount.asp?Action=View* might show the account details, whereas */MyAccount.asp?Action=Edit* allows a user to update her account details. In this example, the *View* and *Edit* functions are layered entry points on the MyAccount.asp page.

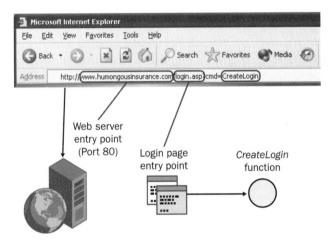

Figure 3-2   Layered entry points in a Web application.

Level of Granularity

To ensure that a threat model is effective, the entry points identified should be granular enough to call out this disparate Web page functionality—but not so granular that they overwhelm the threat modeling process. Ideally, the entry points outlined will be detailed enough to identify all unique threats. Initially, developers might want to build a threat model based on higher-level entry points, and over time, include a more detailed analysis based on more granular entry points.

Relevance to the Threat Model

■   **Who uses the information?**   The information about entry points is primarily used internally among application architects and developers using the threat modeling process, as described in this list.

■ **How is the information collected?**   The system architects and developers provide the list of entry points. Occasionally, additional entry points surface during the data flow modeling of the system. These new entry points are added to the threat model document and analyzed for additional threats.

■ **How is this information used in the rest of the threat model?**   Architects and developers use entry points to prioritize the threat modeling discussion and provide a basis for it. For each entry point, the development team must answer this question: What functionality does the entry point expose? The team then uses this information to identify security-critical actions or data transforms (such as access control checks and protocol parsing) using data flow diagrams (DFDs)—visual representations of how a system processes data. (Chapter 4 discusses DFDs in more detail.) A threat model is considered complete and thorough only if all entry points have been identified and explored.

Data to Collect

When compiling a threat model document, the threat modeling team must gather the following information about the application's entry points:

■ **Numerical ID**   A unique number should be assigned to the entry point the document. This number is used to cross-reference entry points with threats and vulnerabilities later in the threat modeling process. To describe subpoints layered on higher-level entry points, a minor number should be assigned to the higher-level entry point's numerical ID. In a Web application, for example, a particular Web page might have an ID of 4. Thus, functions provided by that Web page to identify sub entry points would have IDs of 4.1, 4.2, and so on.

■ **Name**   A name is a short title for the entry point. The name should be descriptive enough to identify the entry point and its purpose. Some examples include login page, file open function, and control socket.

■ **Description**   The description should explain the processing that occurs at the entry point. For a login page, a description might read: "Takes as input a username and password and returns either a valid login session ID or an Access Denied result if incorrect credentials are supplied. Can also lock the user account if three unsuccessful login attempts are made within a 5-minute period."

■ **Trust levels** The trust levels permitted to access an entry point should be cross-referenced in this section of the threat model document. These trust levels are used to help prioritize later analysis. Entry points with more inclusive trust levels—such as those that allow remote anonymous users to interface with them—are typically higher priority than those with more exclusive access. Trust levels are described in more detail later in this chapter.

Example: Fabrikam Phone 1.0

This section contains one of the three examples of entry points based on the threat model samples used throughout this book. Appendix A contains a complete example of the threat model for the Fabrikam Phone 1.0 application.

The first set of examples, listed in Table 3-1, shows several entry points from Fabrikam, Inc.'s Phone 1.0 application. The trust level number corresponds to the ID value assigned to the trust level. Trust levels are discussed in more detail later in this chapter.

Table 3-1   Entry Points: Fabrikam Phone 1.0

ID	Name	Description	Trust levels
2	Keypad	Used for dialing, entering local access passwords, and other administrative functions	(1) Administrator (2) Long-distance user (3) Local call user (4) Denied user
3	Telephone line	Where the application interfaces with the Public Switched Telephone Network (PSTN)	(5) Remote anonymous user
4	Alphanumeric display	Shows information such as speed-dial numbers, caller ID, and administrative menus	(1) Administrator (2) Long-distance user (3) Local call user (4) Denied user

The Fabrikam Phone 1.0 entry points are consistent with the phone's function. The keypad—used to dial numbers, access administrative functions, and play recorded messages—is an obvious example of a phone's entry point and, therefore, a prime place for an adversary to try to attack the system. To help thwart such attacks, Fabrikam Phone 1.0 employs passwords to restrict access to features such as long-distance calling.

Phone calls and caller ID data travel via the telephone line, making it another entry point of the application. Fabrikam Phone 1.0 has answering-machine functionality as well as remote administrative features. By utilizing the telephone line, remote callers can leave voice messages or try to access the phone's administrative features.

Because this phone's entry points include places where the system transmits unsolicited data, the alphanumeric display should be considered an entry point, too. For example, caller ID information is displayed when a remote caller dials Fabrikam's phone number. An attacker with access to the alphanumeric display can gain access to any company's or individual's name and phone number appearing on the caller ID display, posing an information disclosure threat.

Example: Humongous Insurance Price Quote Website

This section contains one of the three examples of entry points based on the threat model samples used throughout this book. Table 3-2 shows several entry points from the Price Quote Website, including a set of layered entry points. Appendix B contains a complete example of the threat model for the Humongous Insurance Price Quote Website.

Table 3-2   Entry Points: Humongous Insurance Price Quote Website

ID	Name	Description	Trust levels
1	Web server listening port	The port on which the Web server listens. All Web pages are layered on this entry point.	(1) Remote anonymous user (2) Remote user with login credentials (3) Insurance agent (4) Website administrator
1.1	Login page	For users to create a login and to log into the site so that they can request or review an insurance quote.	(1) Remote anonymous user (2) Remote user with login credentials (3) Insurance agent
1.1.1	*CreateLogin* function	Creates a new user login. (Insurance agent logins must be created directly through the database stored procedures.)	(1) Remote anonymous user
1.1.2	*LoginToSite* function	Compares user-supplied credentials to those in the database and creates a new session if the credentials match.	(1) Remote anonymous user (2) Remote user with login credentials (3) Insurance agent

Identifying layered entry points can be useful when a system is built on infrastructure that exposes entry points. The layered entry points of the Humongous Insurance Price Quote Website start with the Web server. The TCP/IP endpoint that the Web server listens on is an entry point that an adversary might try to attack.

On top of the Web server's endpoint, the website contains multiple pages, each of which has several functions. In this example, the login page is the first Web page that a user accessing the site sees. This page has several functions that process the different parameters in a user's request.

The first function, *CreateLogin*, is employed when a user registers with the Humongous Insurance Price Quote Website via a URL such as *http://www .humongousinsurance.com/login.asp?cmd=CreateLogin*. The second function, *LoginToSite*, is employed when a user with a current login account tries to log in to the website. An adversary without an account who wants to gain access to the system could attack the website at either of these entry points.

In this example, some threats might be common to all functions on the login page. Rather than repeat the same threat at each leaf entry point (functions on the login page), the threat is applied to the login page. Thus, it makes sense to layer entry points in this manner. Layering also shows how a system can inherit entry points, and therefore threats, from its infrastructure. In this case, the Price Quote Website inherits threats from the Web server it runs on.

Important   Layering entry points helps the development team organize a threat model. First, it creates a hierarchy that resembles the actual application. Second, it can prevent replication of threats.

Example: A. Datum Corporation Access Control API

This section contains one of the three examples of entry points based on the threat model samples used throughout this book. Table 3-3 shows several entry points from A. Datum Access Control API. These entry points are grouped by methods in classes. Appendix C contains a complete example of the threat model for the Access Control API.

Table 3-3 Entry Points: A. Datum Corporation Access Control API

ID	Name	Description	Trust levels
1	*ACResources*	A class that represents a tree of resources. Child resource nodes in the tree inherit the access control list of their parent by default.	(1) The program using the API (2) A user with unknown access to a resource (3) A user with read access to a resource (4) A user with write access to a resource
1.1	*Add*	Adds a resource to the tree at the specified path.	(1) The program using the API
1.2	*Remove*	Removes the resource at the specified path.	(1) The program using the API
1.3	*Get*	Returns the resource at the specified path.	(1) The program using the API (2) A user with unknown access to a resource (3) A user with read access to a resource (4) A user with write access to a resource
1.4	*GetRoot*	Gets the root resource.	(1) The program using the API
1.5	*GetChildren*	Gets the child resources at the specified path.	(1) The program using the API
1.6	*GetParent*	Gets the parent resource of the specified path.	(1) The program using the API
1.8	*SetPathResolver*	Sets an optional path resolver that maps paths supplied to the class from an arbitrary form to the normalized form used by the *ACResources* class.	(1) The program using the API

The A. Datum Access Control API example features grouped entry points. Grouped entry points are particularly useful when the threat model is created for a library or other reusable software component. For object-oriented systems, entry points are often methods in a class. Each group of entry points usually corresponds to the classes in the library.

The A. Datum example shows method entry points in the *ACResources* class, which is used to store a tree of resources that users can be granted access to. Most of the functions in this class, such as *Add*, *Remove*, *GetRoot*, *GetChildren*, *GetParent*, and *SetPathResolver*, are used only by the application that uses the API. The trust levels reflect that these functions are internally used. The *Get* method, however, can process data supplied by an unknown user. For example, if the system controls access to files on the file system, a user could try to write to a file. That file's pathname is passed to the *Get* function so that the system can check the user's access rights. Thus, the *Get* function processes data from users, not just from the program that uses the API. The program relies on the *Get* method to process the potentially malicious data securely. The *Get* method must be designed and implemented to protect against the threat of an adversary providing malformed data.

Determining Which Assets Are of Interest

Assets are resources that the system must protect from incorrect or unauthorized use. For example, as Figure 3-3 shows, the common assets of an office building include business equipment such as computers and fax machines, corporate data such as that stored in file cabinets and computer systems, and the free soft drinks provided to employees. An adversary who obtains access to these assets could cause financial damage to the company. Obviously, some assets are more valuable than others. Threats targeting the corporate data carry a different level of risk than threats targeting the soda.

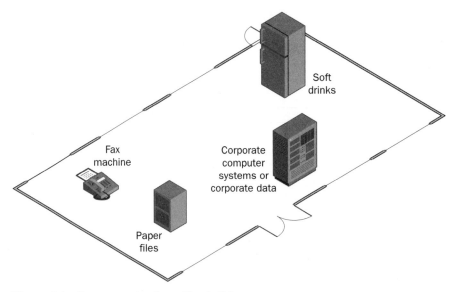

Figure 3-3   Some assets of an office building.

Abstract Assets

Physical assets such as business equipment and soft drinks are generally easy to understand and identify. However, not all assets are homogeneous; nor are they always concrete. Some assets, such as the following examples, are *abstract*:

- **The safety of the employees who work there.**   The mere presence of an unauthorized person in the building could damage the employees' sense of security.

- **The company's reputation.**   If an adversary breaks into a company's website and defaces the home page, the company might be considered a safety risk even if no customer data is compromised. In other words, if this company's products or services are purchased because they are perceived to be secure, the defacement could change how customers see the company even if its most critical assets were never at risk.

- **The availability of resources.**   Consider a peer-to-peer network in which the network is closed to outsiders (that is, only authorized nodes are allowed to join the network). Because the network is peer-to-peer, with no central server that all nodes connect to, ensuring that all nodes can communicate with all other nodes can be difficult. An adversary could cause a denial of service by disrupting connectivity. Thus, connectivity—in this case, the ability for nodes to communicate with each other, ensuring that the network exists as a single graph rather than as several disjoint graphs—is an asset.

Assets are the reason an adversary attacks a system. As the examples in this chapter have shown, assets are clearly valuable to both the system and the adversary: the architects and developers of the system must provide safeguards to ensure that their assets are not used improperly or by unauthorized external entities, while the adversary tries to gain access to or affect these assets in some manner.

Important   A threat cannot exist unless it corresponds to at least one asset of interest to an adversary.

Transitive Assets

Assets can be *transitive* through their relationship with other assets. A component that is accessible via an entry point in a system often interacts with other components in the system. This first component can act as a gateway to the functionality and assets of the other components. The assets of the other components are considered the transitive assets of this first component.

An example of a component with transitive assets is a mechanism in the system that is used as a checkpoint. For example, consider a component that uses an access control mechanism to check entries on a resource to see whether a user has access rights to that resource. Even though the mechanism does not interact directly with that resource (it simply checks the access control list on behalf of another component), it transitively takes on the resource as an asset. This is because the calling component determines whether to grant access based solely on the information returned by the access control mechanism.

Assessing Risk to Assets

To determine the risk of a realized threat, or a *vulnerability*, consider the damage an adversary could cause if she gets her hands on a particular asset. For example, in a peer-to-peer application, a loss of connectivity results in a denial of service. In an office building, an adversary gaining access to corporate data results in information disclosure. Defining assets is important not only in determining threats, but also in understanding what an adversary would gain by realizing those threats.

In some systems, it is easier to identify assets if they are grouped according to the part of the system they belong to. This is particularly useful in Web applications and other multiuser systems. For example, the assets of a Web commerce application that processes user orders could include the users' credit card numbers, the purchase invoices, and the website availability. These assets might belong to the user, application, and server categories, respectively. Categorizing assets in this manner can make the threat model more thorough, as well as ensure that significant types of assets are not missed altogether.

Relevance to the Threat Model

- **Who uses the information?** The threat modeling team uses the information when identifying threats. When analyzing security-critical processing, points where an asset is referenced should be scrutinized. The assets are the targets of threats to the system.

- **How is the information collected?**   Many assets are identified when discussing system functionality, use scenarios, and other background information. Questions to ask include: Does the system have access to any resources that an external entity could not normally access? Which aspects of the system are critical to proper functionality? What is the purpose of this system?

- **How is this information used in the rest of the threat model?**   Assets are used during threat identification to identify an adversary's goals.

Data to Collect

When creating a threat model, the development team must gather the following information about the assets to protect:

- **Numerical ID**   A unique number should be assigned to the asset. This ID is used to cross-reference entry points with threats and vulnerabilities later in the threat modeling process. This is discussed further in Chapter 5.

- **Name**   This is a short title for the asset. The name should be descriptive enough to identify the asset—for example, administrator process token, access to files, and graph connectivity.

- **Description**   The description should provide an explanation of why the asset needs to be protected. For administrative process privileges, the description might be: "The application runs under administrative privileges but has lower-privileged clients. Because the application has unlimited rights and the clients do not, an adversary who causes the application to perform unintended operations achieves an elevation of privilege." (Elevation of privilege, or gaining the ability to perform a task previously restricted, will be discussed shortly.)

- **Trust levels**   The trust levels that are normally allowed to access or otherwise interact with the asset should be cross-referenced here. The trust levels help determine the risk associated with system vulnerabilities. Trust levels are described in more detail later in this chapter.

Example: Fabrikam Phone 1.0

This section contains one of three examples that show how assets are specific to each system. These examples also illustrate both heterogeneous and transitive assets. Table 3-4 shows several assets from the Fabrikam Phone 1.0 application. Appendix A contains a complete example of the threat model for this application.

Table 3-4 Assets: Fabrikam Phone 1.0

ID	Name	Description	Trust level
1	Speed-dial list	Contains the names and numbers of frequently used contacts.	(1) Administrator (2) Long-distance user (3) Local call user
2	Caller ID	Provides information about incoming callers	(1) Administrator (2) Long-distance user (3) Local call user
3	Access to the PSTN	The Phone 1.0 application indirectly protects access to the PSTN.	(1) Administrator (2) Long-distance user (3) Local call user
4	Long-distance calling	Phone 1.0 has optional lockout for long-distance calling so that only authorized users can make long-distance calls.	(1) Administrator (2) Long-distance user

For the Fabrikam Phone 1.0, the speed-dial list is an asset; it includes personal data (names and telephone numbers) that could be subject to disclosure or tampering. Caller ID information is also an asset. As with the speed-dial list, the caller ID feature can disclose sensitive information. For example, a company might not want to disclose that it is receiving numerous calls from creditors.

Furthermore, because the Phone 1.0 includes access control features that can block a phone user from dialing local or long-distance, the assets include access to the PSTN and the ability to make a long-distance call. To reduce charges for outgoing calls, a company might want to prevent calls that are not work related. If E.T. were to phone home from the corporate lobby, not only would he successfully elevate his access privileges, he also would likely cause the company a denial of service by racking up a staggering phone bill the company cannot afford.

Example: Humongous Insurance Price Quote Website

This section contains one of three examples that show how assets are specific to each system. Table 3-5 shows several assets from the Price Quote Website. Appendix B contains a complete example of the threat.

Table 3-5   Assets: Humongous Insurance Price Quote Website

ID	Name	Description	Trust level
1	User and agent	Assets that relate to a user or an insurance agent.	None
1.1	User's login data	The user's credentials: username and password.	(2) Remote user with login credentials (5) Database server administrator
1.2	User's personal data	The personal data that the user enters, such as contact information, assets, and the like.	(2) Remote user with login credentials (3) Insurance agent
3	Process	Assets that relate to the process running on the website.	N/A
3.1	Ability to execute code as the identity of the Web server	Web pages on the site execute code using the security token of the Web server.	(4) Website administrator (6) Web server process identity
4	Application	Assets that relate to the Web application.	N/A
4.1	Access to back-end database	The ability to interact with the database that stores user data, insurance quotes, and login credentials.	(5) Database server administrator (6) Web server process identity (7) Database server process identity

Assets for a system are often heterogeneous, as illustrated by the assets of the Humongous Insurance Price Quote Website. For example, disclosing a user's login data (username and password) could elevate the privileges of another user. Elevation of privilege occurs when a user gains the ability to perform a task previously restricted, without necessarily gaining administrative privileges. A user who can log in to a website as another user has elevated her privileges to those of that other user.

Another asset represented in Table 3-5, the user's personal data, is an example of information subject to privacy concerns. All data that is governed by federal privacy legislation or regulations should be included in the threat model as an asset. This data will be the target of information disclosure threats.

Access to the back-end database is an asset exposed indirectly through the Web pages that use the database to store and retrieve data, and directly by the database itself. An adversary can attempt to access the database and run arbitrary commands, resulting in elevation of privilege, information disclosure, or tampering with the data stored in the database.

The ability to execute code as the process identity of the Web server is both an asset of the Web server and a transitive asset. Because the Web pages execute within the Web server process, the website takes the process token as an asset. An adversary who can change the functionality of the website—for example, by replacing one of the Web pages—can execute code as the identity of the Web server process.

> **Note** In the examples above, trust levels are not cross-referenced with "User and Agent," "Process," and "Application." This is because these entries are used as groupings of assets according to the area of the application that owns them, as noted earlier in this chapter.

Example: A. Datum Access Control API

This section contains one of three examples that show how assets are specific to each system. Table 3-6 shows several assets from the Access Control API. Appendix C contains a complete example of the threat model.

Table 3-6 Assets: A. Datum Access Control API

ID	Name	Description	Trust level
1	Process	Assets that relate to the process that the library is running in.	None
1.1	Ability to execute arbitrary code as the identity of the process	The library executes in the process space of the program using it. Buffer overflows and similar implementation issues in the library could allow a user to execute arbitrary code.	(1) The program using the API

Table 3-6   Assets: A. Datum Access Control API

ID	Name	Description	Trust level
2	Library	Assets that relate specifically to the library.	None
2.1	Read access to resources	The ability to read from a resource.	(3) A user with read access to a resource
2.2	Write access to resources	The ability to write to a resource.	(4) A user with write access to a resource

The first two assets of the A. Datum Access Control API are examples of transitive assets. The API does not give the user read access or write access to the resource. Instead, the application that uses the API to look up the user's privileges set for the resource does this. However, because the application makes the decision based solely on the result from the API, the API must take read and write access to resources as transitive assets.

The Access Control API is a library that runs in the process space of an application and has the ability to run arbitrary code. Thus, one asset of the API is the ability to run this arbitrary code. An attacker could try to gain this ability in various ways, including finding a buffer overflow that allows code injection or possibly replacing the on-disk image of the library or a library that the API relies on.

Trust Levels

Trust levels, or access categories, represent the set of rights given to an external entity based on the system's knowledge about that entity. Trust levels group external entities into logical categories. For example, if a system's trust levels correspond to user groups, those groups are based on authentication. Trust levels are applied to external entities at system entry points to safeguard assets. An organization uses trust levels to define which external entities can interact with an entry point and which entities should have legitimate privileges to any given asset.

In an office building, the front-door entry point might have several trust levels with access to the building, such as executives, security officers, employees, and maintenance personnel. Entry point trust levels for external entities might also account for denials of access, depending on where the access check occurs. If the access check occurs once the building's front door is open (for example, with a security guard checking ID badges), the front-door trust levels should also account for people without company ID badges. People without these credentials would normally be denied access by the security guard once they are inside the building. Building visitors without ID badges (employees who forgot their badge that day or people who are not employees) who manage to enter the front door by sneaking past the security guard will have successfully elevated their privileges.

Trust levels help prioritize the access types granted and denied in an organization's threat model documentation. For example, if access to an entry point requires administrative-level credentials, that entry point might be deemed less of a security risk than an entry point that grants access to remote, anonymous users. The more anonymous an entry point's users are, the more potential adversaries that entry point has.

As with other data points in threat modeling, trust levels are not homogeneous. Although they often correspond to authentication groups, they also can correspond to other types of groups. For example, a network socket on a Web server would have an access category of remote anonymous users—users who can access the Web server's network. Although such users have not provided authentication credentials to the Web server, their trust level does imply a distinct level of access.

Relevance to the Threat Model

- **Who uses the information?**   The threat modeling team uses trust levels to determine high-risk entry points and prioritize the various aspects of the security discussion. The team can also use trust levels when discussing assets. Trust levels are particularly relevant in analyzing potential elevation-of-privilege attacks.

- **How is the information collected?**   The architects of the system should have the trust level information readily available. This information is simply an enumeration of who should and should not have access to each entry point or protected resource.

- **How is the information used in the rest of the threat model?**   Trust levels help prioritize discussion of granting and denying access to external entities. Trust levels are also used when discussing mitigation and risk. For example, one could argue that a buffer overflow at an entry point that requires administrative-level privileges is not a high security risk because the administrator would not gain access to any protected resources that he does not already have access to. (Of course, this depends on the threat model's definition of *administrator* and is specific to each individual system.)

Data to Collect

When creating a threat model, the development team must gather the following information about an application's trust levels:

- **Numerical ID**   A unique number should be assigned to the trust level. This ID is used to cross-reference trust levels with entry points and assets.

- **Name**   This name is a short title of the trust level and should be descriptive enough to distinguish the external entities granted this trust level. Some examples include administrators, users with write privileges to the local file system, and remote anonymous users.

- **Description**   The description should provide a more specific explanation of the trust level. For users with write privileges to the local file system, this description might read: "Users who have write privileges to the configuration directory, which can include remote users if file sharing is enabled."

Example: Fabrikam Phone 1.0

This section contains one of three examples of application trust levels based on the threat model samples used in this book. Table 3-7 shows several trust levels from the Fabrikam Phone 1.0 application. Appendix A contains a complete example of the threat model.

Table 3-7   Trust Levels: Fabrikam Phone 1.0

ID	Name	Description
1	Administrator	The Phone 1.0 application administrator has access to all features and can bypass all security checks.
2	Long-distance user	Phone 1.0 can be configured to restrict long-distance calling. The long-distance user is a phone user who is allowed to make long-distance calls.
3	Local call user	The local call user can place only outgoing local calls.
4	Denied user	Phone 1.0 can be configured to deny access to the phone without the use of a password.

Fabrikam Phone 1.0 can block users from accessing certain features of the phone system based on the password that the user inputs. The various trust levels include administrator, long-distance user, and local call user. These trust levels shown here have distinct differences from the assets described earlier in

Table 3-4. For example, one asset—the ability to call long-distance—should be accessible only to administrators and long-distance users. Local call users should not have access to this asset.

Looking back to the entry points for Fabrikam Phone 1.0 (shown in Table 3-1), the administrators, long-distance users, local call users, and the denied users can all access the keypad. Although the denied user should not be able to access assets beyond the entry point (such as making a local call), the user can still access the actual entry point. For example, a person who does not have a password for using the phone can still try to type one using the keypad.

Example: Humongous Insurance Price Quote Website

This section contains one of three examples of application trust levels based on the threat model samples used in this book. Table 3-8 shows several trust levels from the Price Quote Website. Appendix B contains a complete example of the threat model.

Table 3-8 Trust Levels: Humongous Insurance Price Quote Website

ID	Name	Description
1	Remote anonymous user	A user who has connected to the website but has not yet provided legitimate credentials.
2	Remote user with login credentials	A user who has created an account and has entered valid login credentials.
3	Insurance agent	The insurance agent has login credentials that allow him to view the quote review page.
4	Website administrator	The website administrator can configure the insurance quote website.
5	Database server administrator	The database administrator can access and modify the database and the information in it.
6	Web server process identity	Used to authenticate the Web server to the database when storing or retrieving information and serves as the identity that all actions taken by the Web server process occur under.
7	Database server process identity	The account that the database server process runs as, represented by its process token. The database process has all of the access and privileges that correspond to this token.

Trust levels for the Humongous Insurance Price Quote Website correspond to users who access the site, administrators of the infrastructure components, and the process identities of the running processes. For example, until a user is authenticated through the login page, she is considered a remote anonymous user. This is typically the most inclusive trust level for an application.

Users with login credentials are another category of trust level. They have access to their account information only. An insurance agent has different access—he can view any user's data in order to service requests. The website and database administrators are not accounts in the Web application; they are accounts in the host operating system that are allowed to configure the Web server and database server, respectively. These can be different than the accounts that the Web server process and database server process execute as, so Web server process identity and database server process identity are separate trust levels.

Example: A. Datum Access Control API

This section contains one of three examples of application trust levels based on the threat model samples used in this book. Table 3-9 shows several trust levels from the Access Control API. Appendix C contains a complete example of the threat model.

Table 3-9   Trust Levels: A. Datum Access Control API

ID	Name	Description
1	The program using the API	The process identity of the program that uses the library is the direct user of the API.
2	A user with unknown access to a resource	The process using the library passes a user's request for access to resources to the API. The user might have unknown access to the resource.
3	A user with read access to a resource	The process using the library passes a user's request for access to resources to the API. The user might have read access to the resource.
4	A user with write access to a resource	The process using the library passes a user's request for access to resources to the API. The user might have write access to the resource.

Examples of trust levels for the A. Datum Access Control API include the program that uses the API and users with unknown access rights to a resource. Trust levels define either the direct consumer of the entry point or the source of the data supplied to it. The program using the A. Datum Access Control API is the direct consumer of the API, while a user with unknown access rights can indirectly supply the API with data (such as a string containing a pathname for a resource).

Assets for the A. Datum Access Control API are also cross-referenced with trust levels. For example, write access to a particular resource should be restricted to users who have been granted write access for that resource.

Summary

To begin the threat modeling process, the development team must first enumerate the entry points, assets, and trust levels of the application or system. This is required for the team to understand how an adversary might approach the application to achieve a particular goal.

The threat modeling process enables the team to develop an understanding of the security risks associated with the application they are creating. To do so, the team must evaluate the data flow through the application at every entry point, for every trust level, and with respect to every asset.

Next, Chapter 4 will consider external dependencies, implementation assumptions, and use scenarios. It will also demonstrate how to build a graphical representation of the data flow through the system.

Constraining and Modeling the Application

To construct a threat model, development teams must fully understand the system they want to secure. To better understand a system, an application's development team must employ the two-stage process covered in this chapter:

- Gather relevant background information to bound the scope of application analysis.

- Model the application to understand processing and data flows.

Both stages serve several purposes. First, they constrain the threat model to a known system in a supported configuration. Second, they ensure that the threat modeling team obtains the necessary information to complete the threat modeling documentation. And third, they provide a background for the threat model that will be used later by reviewers.

Although this part of threat modeling can be tedious, it can save time in the long run by scoping the threat model. In addition, this stage of threat modeling preserves assumptions, dependencies, and data flow characteristics so that the threat model is still meaningful in the future. Without this information, threat models often appear as though constructed in a vacuum, prompting questions such as: "What about this configuration?" "Does a change in this other application affect the security of this one?" "How did this application work?"

This chapter presents data points that are useful in the threat modeling process. As with other aspects of threat modeling, different development environments will often dictate the data that is collected. This chapter covers the following topics:

- Gathering background information
- Modeling the application

> **Note**   This chapter uses the data flow diagramming technique for the application modeling process. Some development teams use other process-diagramming techniques in creating software specifications and already might have invested significant amounts of time in these illustrations. Thus, such development teams should leverage their existing diagrams as much as possible.

Gathering Relevant Background Information

Threat modeling an application will require discussions with architects and developers, investigations into the application's design and implementation, verification of interapplication dependencies, and more. This entire process must be bounded to be completed on time and as thoroughly as possible. Therefore, before the threat modeling team can enumerate threats, it must collect background information. Armed with this information, development teams can steer their discussions away from tangents that are irrelevant to the threat model being created. Background information is divided into five categories:

- Use scenarios
- External dependencies
- External security notes
- Internal security notes
- Implementation assumptions

Threat Model Documentation

An important aspect to the threat modeling process is documenting the findings and analysis. Chapters 3 through 5 show examples in table format of information collected during threat modeling. These data points (including the DFDs used for flow analysis) should be collated into a threat model document. Much as an application's specification should exist in some form of document, the threat model should also be preserved as a document.

The threat model describes the system's threat profile and the threat model document preserves the work that was done during threat modeling. This document serves multiple purposes:

- It reveals how thorough the analysis of the system was for security reviews of the system.

- It ensures that threats are actually investigated by requiring that appropriate mitigation information is included.

- It is used during security testing to prioritize testing and provide a basis for the work plan.

- It provides a way to judge the relative security of the system, particularly when threat models of previous versions exist.

- It contains the background information that new members of the development team require to gain an understanding of the security issues facing the application.

- It is used during root cause analysis of externally reported vulnerabilities.

The exact format of the threat model document is not critical. What is essential, however, is that the appropriate data is captured. Threat model examples of three fictitious systems are shown in full in the appendixes. These examples are presented in tables similar to those presented in Chapters 3 through 5. Other formats are acceptable, especially if they correspond to existing formats such as software specifications in a particular development environment.

Use Scenarios

A *use scenario* explains how the system is or is not intended to be used in deployment. It can be expressed in terms of configuration or in terms of security goals and nongoals—that is, security problems that the system is not designed to cope with. Use scenarios help bound the threat modeling document by describing the threats that were considered during the security design of the system. Use scenarios can also explain situations in which the security can be compromised if the system is deployed in an unsupported configuration.

> **Note** Throughout the threat modeling process, consider how the information collected relates to the particular system being modeled. Keep in mind that the word *system* can mean anything from a Web server to a string class in a library. *System* is simply a generic term for something that exposes functionality to external entities. In this case, *deployment* is a generic term for a configuration or method of use for the system.

The office building scenario presented in Chapter 3 provides an example of a *supported use scenario* that could mitigate repudiation threats (threats where an attacker has plausible deniability of wrongdoing). In this use scenario, the building should have its card-key access system enabled. If this system is disabled, the office building cannot detect the identity of people passing in and out of its doors.

In the same office building example, an *unsupported use scenario* would be the office building failing to protect against human threats, such as tailgating (when people without card keys follow those with card keys into the building). If the building's card-key access is enabled, a valid user can still gain entry and an adversary can still sneak in before the door closes, as shown in Figure 4-1.

Preventing tailgaters from entering the office building is a nongoal because it cannot be solved in a practical manner. Thus, this threat can be resolved by linking to this use scenario, even though the threat is valid and would otherwise result in a vulnerability. In other words, the threat is recognized, but because it is a security nongoal of the building, true mitigation is not pursued. Of course, mantraps (or other mechanisms that allow only one person through an entryway at a time), guards, and cameras could also be used to prevent tailgating if doing so is deemed a supported use scenario.

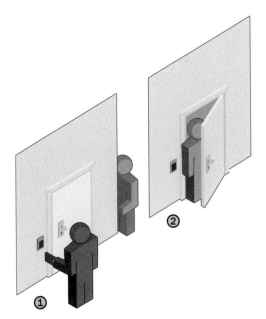

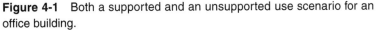

Figure 4-1   Both a supported and an unsupported use scenario for an office building.

> **Important**   Use scenarios can be used to mitigate threats to the system. A use scenario that is violated or ignored will often manifest a vulnerability. Be careful to consider common deployments. It is not advisable to claim that a threat is mitigated because it exists in an unsupported use scenario if that use scenario is or will be a common scenario for end users.

Another example of an unsupported use scenario is opening windows for air circulation instead of using the building's heating, ventilating, and air conditioning (HVAC) system. Despite the potential energy savings, the threat of an adversary using a window that has been left open to gain entry into the building becomes a valid vulnerability, as depicted in Figure 4-2.

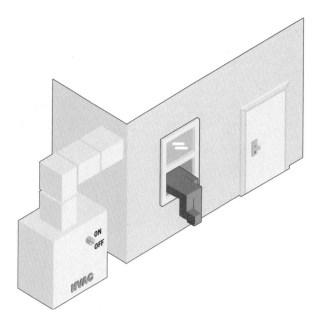

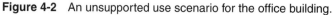

Figure 4-2 An unsupported use scenario for the office building.

Use scenarios deal with deployment considerations that directly affect the security of the system being modeled. Although use scenarios can apply to any system, they most often apply to end-to-end applications that are used with little or no integration work. Frameworks such as libraries, components, or other software pieces integrated into larger applications typically have fewer use scenarios and more external security notes. (External security notes, which provide security-related information to users interacting with the system being modeled, will be discussed later in this section.)

Relevance to the Threat Model

- **Who uses the information?** Use scenarios are used by the threat modeling team to limit the scope of the analysis. Architects typically must sign off on the individual use scenarios for the threat model to be valid. Later, the security test team can use these scenarios when conducting a penetration test (a test of a system's implementation that attempts various attack paths), either to verify the scenarios' validity or prove that they are not consistent with actual deployment.

- **How is the information collected?** The information is best provided by the architect of the system being modeled. End users of the system might also have input about how the system is being used.

■ **How is this information used in the rest of the threat model?** Use scenarios can limit the discussion by describing situations that will not be considered—in other words, scenarios outside the "safe" use of the system. During threat analysis, use scenarios can be utilized as the mitigation for conditions. For example, a threat might be a valid vulnerability only if the system is used in an unsupported, or "unsafe," scenario.

Data to Collect

When specifying use scenarios in a threat modeling document, the development team should gather and record the following pieces of information:

■ **Numerical ID** A unique number should be assigned to the use scenario. This number can be used to cross-reference threats that are mitigated because they apply only to configurations outside the supported use scenarios.

■ **Description** The description should explain the configuration and whether it is supported or unsupported—for example: "Security of usernames and passwords in transit on the network is only supported when Secure Sockets Layer (SSL) is enabled. If it is disabled, the system cannot provide protection against credential sniffing on the network."

Example: Fabrikam Phone 1.0

Table 4-1 shows two use scenarios for Fabrikam's Phone 1.0 application; both scenarios document issues that are beyond the control of the application. The first use scenario for Fabrikam's Phone 1.0 application is used to scope the threat model by pointing out that the PSTN is outside the control—and thus the security boundary—of the phone. Therefore, the PSTN must be considered a potentially hostile source of data. The second use scenario shown here notes that the phone was not designed to protect against direct physical attacks. Threats such as an adversary opening the phone handset and installing a voice tap are beyond the scope of the threat model.

Table 4-1   Use Scenarios: Fabrikam Phone 1.0

ID	Description
1	Fabrikam Phone 1.0 will be connected to the Public Switched Telephone Network (PSTN). The security of this network is beyond the control of Phone 1.0.
3	Fabrikam did not design Phone 1.0 to withstand attacks against the physical device.

Example: Humongous Insurance Price Quote Website

Table 4-2 shows several use scenarios from the Humongous Insurance Price Quote Website; this table documents network deployment scenarios for the website. These use scenarios outline how the website should be deployed in a network environment. For example, the website should be deployed on a server that is secure and has the latest security patches. In addition, the threat model assumes that the only TCP ports exposed to the Internet are the HTTP (80) and HTTPS (443) ports. Furthermore, the threat model assumes that the network between the Web server and the database server is private, reducing the need to encrypt the network traffic as long as insider threats of sniffing sensitive data on the wire are considered out of scope.

Table 4-2   Use Scenarios: Humongous Insurance Price Quote Website

ID	Description
1	The Price Quote Website will be installed on a Web server that has been secured to current industry guidelines. Current security patches for the Web server must be maintained.
4	The Web server should be protected from direct access (except for the HTTP and HTTPS ports) from the Internet by a firewall.
5	Communication between the Web server and the database server should be over a private network.

Example: A. Datum Access Control API

Table 4-3 shows a use scenario from the A. Datum Access Control API; it describes that the *ACADatumOSFilePathResolver* should be used only on A. Datum Operating System 1.0. In other words, if this class is used on another operating system, threats against the library will not be considered because critical operations such as path resolution semantics will likely differ and could cause security issues.

Table 4-3   Use Scenario: A. Datum Access Control API

ID	Description
1	The *ACADatumOSFilePathResolver* class is an implementation of *IACPathResolver* that resolves path names on A. Datum Operating System 1.0 and will not work for other operating systems. Using this implementation on other operating systems could result in incorrect mapping of path names to the A. Datum Access Control API canonical form.

External Dependencies

External dependencies are requirements levied on systems outside the system being modeled. They can be dependencies on a certain behavior or a specification compliance in an external system that, if disregarded, could turn threats into valid vulnerabilities. Typically, the development team has little or no control over external dependencies.

The office building in Figure 4-3 has an external dependency on the power grid it connects to. If power from the grid is lost, the card-key access system will be off line. In addition, local fire codes might dictate that the system "fail open." That is, if power is lost, the door must unlock so that people inside the building can escape and firefighters can get in. In this case, loss of power makes the threat of an adversary gaining access to the building during such a condition a valid vulnerability.

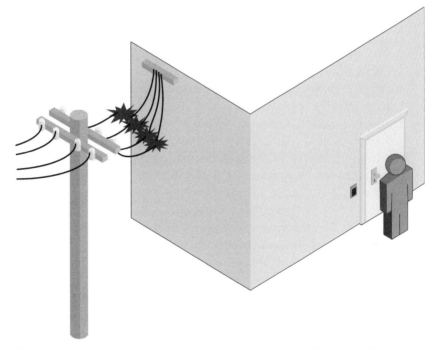

Figure 4-3   An external dependency on the power grid of an office building.

External dependencies can be used to mitigate threats in such cases. The threat of an adversary gaining entry when the building loses power is valid, but it might not be feasible to do anything about it because of fire codes. Of course, it might be possible to mitigate the threat through other means, such as posting security guards or using a backup generator (if the fire codes allow this).

Note The threat modeling team should be critical when using external dependencies to mitigate threats. This practice is often not the most appropriate because it places the responsibility of mitigation on components outside the control of the development team. If the dependency is not validated, the system will not be truly secure. Compounding this is the observation that a significant number of vulnerabilities occur at component and application boundaries due to miscommunication or misunderstanding of behavior.

In software systems, external dependencies often describe systemwide functions such as algorithm consistency. For example, if two systems both normalize a string of text and take action based on the result, it might be important that the normalized representation is the same across both systems. Consider a Web server that implements access control to Web pages based on the virtual path from the Web root. That Web server must perform path normalization on the request uniform resource identifier (URI) that the client sends and match its virtual path to determine access control. If that check succeeds, the Web server might prepend a physical root to the path and instruct the file system to open the file. The file system driver might perform its own path normalization.

In this case, it could be possible to construct a request that is normalized differently by the Web server and the file system. In other words, the Web server grants access because it believes the file system will return a certain file, but when the file system parses the file name, the name normalizes to something different. Thus, the Web server has an external dependency on the file system in that the file path normalization routines must match. The threat of an adversary constructing a malicious request that is interpreted differently has been a valid vulnerability in Web servers in the past.

Alternate Data Streams and Microsoft Internet Information Server

Microsoft Knowledge Base article 188806 describes a specific vulnerability that resulted from an inconsistency in an external dependency for Microsoft Internet Information Server (IIS). In this case, the dependency that IIS had on the underlying file system was consistency in path normalization routines. Both IIS and the underlying Microsoft Windows NT file system, NTFS, performed normalization on the path that a user requested. The problem was that the normalization differed, causing IIS to return server-side source code rather than running that code.

NTFS supports multiple data streams in a file. Put simply, this allows one or more sets of data to be associated with a single file. The default data stream is normally accessed by requesting the file name, such as Sample.txt. But this data stream can also be accessed by explicitly selecting the data from the default data stream: Sample.txt::$DATA.

Vulnerable versions of IIS did not support the concept of alternate data streams. This resulted in the ability of an adversary to retrieve source code for server-processed pages, such as Active Server Pages (ASP). Consider the legitimate request *http://www.fabrikam.com/process.asp*. When IIS parses this request, it will recognize the .asp extension of the file and know that ASP should run the page server-side and return the result. However, a malicious request such as *http://www.fabrikam.com/process.asp::$DATA* would not be recognized as an ASP page by IIS because the extension would be .asp::$DATA. Because this does not match the expected extension, it will be assumed that the page is static data rather than server-side code. IIS would read the file from disk and return it to the user.

Obviously, understanding how a Web application works can be useful to an adversary. In addition, developers will unfortunately often place sensitive information such as database passwords in server-side script. If exploited, this vulnerability could result in disclosure of valuable company information.

Relevance to the Threat Model

- **Who uses the information?**   External dependencies are primarily used by the threat modeling team to validate assumptions between systems being modeled. Identifying, documenting, and investigating external dependencies can ensure that disparate systems and groups do not create inconsistent assumptions at component and system boundaries that lead to vulnerabilities.

- **How is the information collected?**   The system architects and often its developers should identify external systems that the application depends on. Furthermore, they should characterize the functionality of the external systems that is used, thus providing a list of dependencies.

- **How is this information used in the rest of the threat model?**   External dependencies result in action items that must be resolved with the target system's team before a threat model can be considered valid. These action items validate cross-system assumptions that, if incorrect, might result in vulnerabilities.

Data to Collect

Development teams documenting a threat model should gather the following information about external dependencies:

- **Numerical ID**   A unique number should be assigned to the external dependency. This number can be used to cross-reference threats that are mitigated because they are beyond the control of the system being modeled.

- **Description**   A description of the dependency should be given— for example: "Path normalization needs to be consistent with that of the underlying operating system and file system."

- **External security note reference**   In environments where threat modeling is tightly integrated, external dependencies on other components within the application can be cross-referenced with external security notes from the referenced external component. (External security notes are described later in this section.)

Example: Fabrikam Phone 1.0

Table 4-4 shows an external dependency for the Fabrikam Phone 1.0 application; it states that the phone is dependent on the PSTN for power. Because this particular phone uses volatile memory to store messages and configuration, this dependency has the potential for a denial of service.

Table 4-4   External Dependency: Fabrikam Phone 1.0

ID	Description
1	Fabrikam Phone 1.0 depends on the PSTN for providing power. There is a two-day power cell in Phone 1.0 that provides backup power should the power provided by the PSTN fail.

Example: Humongous Insurance Price Quote Website

Table 4-5 shows an external dependency from the Humongous Insurance Price Quote Website. It documents that the session management (the mechanism used to maintain the logged-in state of a user between Web requests) is implemented by the Web server, but that the website relies on this session management to be secure. Insecure session management could allow an adversary to take control of another user's session, resulting in an elevation of privilege.

Table 4-5   External Dependency: Humongous Insurance Price Quote Website

ID	Description
4	The Price Quote Website depends on the session management of the Web server to be secure. If the session is insecure, an adversary might be able to hijack another user's session.

Example: A. Datum Access Control API

Table 4-6 shows an external dependency from the A. Datum Access Control API. It documents that the path normalization in the *ACADatumOSFilePathResolver* class needs to work similarly to that of the underlying operating system. This dependency would be resolved by cross-referencing it with the published normalization routine for the operating system.

Table 4-6   External Dependency: A. Datum Access Control API

ID	Description
1	The *ACADatumOSFilePathResolver* depends on the file paths in A. Datum Operating System 1.0 being resolved the same way as implemented in this class. If the file paths resolve differently in the operating system, the mapping that the *ACADatumOSFilePathResolver* performs could result in an incorrect resource being checked for access. In the worst-case scenario, this could allow an adversary to access a file he could not normally access.

External Security Notes

External security notes are the counterpart of external dependencies. They provide security-relevant information to users that interface with the system being modeled. This information can take the form of warnings against potential misuse that, although not presently a vulnerability in the system being modeled, might lead to a vulnerability in another system if not used correctly. Or the information provided by external security notes can take the form of guarantees that the system makes to users.

> **Note** In contrast with use scenarios, which discuss configuration and deployment, external security notes provide integration information. An end user likely would need to know about this information to construct a secure application when building a larger system from that being modeled.

In the office building example, an external security note could be the service-level agreement (SLA) that the power company has with the office, as shown in Figure 4-4. This agreement provides certain guaranties that the power company makes about power continuity and repair. In this example, the SLA with the power company guaranties only 95 percent uptime, which could lead to some denial-of-service threats. To mitigate those threats, the office building administrators might choose to use a power generator to back up critical systems. Of course, the cost of installing and supporting the generator must be taken into account; it might not be worth the cost to mitigate the 5 percent downtime.

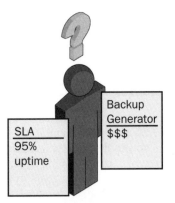

Figure 4-4 Using a backup generator to mitigate denial-of-service threats resulting from an office's building's SLA with the power company.

External security notes might be information that is proactively entered into the threat model document or information that is documented in response to another system having an external dependency on the system. For example, a threat model for the file system could contain the specification for how file names are normalized so that the normalization routine in a Web server can be cross-referenced.

External security notes can also be used as the basis for security notes in product documentation. This is particularly relevant for libraries or other components that provide programmatic interfaces.

Relevance to the Threat Model

- **Who uses the information?** The information is primarily consumed by users whose systems in turn depend upon this system. Those users can validate dependencies based on this information or request explanation of functionality to be added.

- **How is the information collected?** During the threat modeling process, potential misuses of externally supplied functionality are often identified. This information should be proactively included in the threat model. In addition, external dependencies on this system can force investigations that result in information being added to this table.

- **How is this information used in the rest of the threat model?** External security notes are used to validate external dependencies. In addition, external security notes can sometimes be used as mitigation for threats. In this case, the threat is mitigated through end-user education rather than through design or implementation changes. Note that mitigating in this manner places security in the hands of the end user, which is usually not advisable.

Data to Collect

Development teams documenting a threat model should gather the following information about external security notes:

- **Numerical ID** A unique number should be given to the external security note. This number is used as an index when external dependencies in other threat models need to be cross-referenced.

- **Description** This is an explanation of the issue at hand, or a link to the location where the information is stored when algorithms or other complex issues must be described. For example: "Users need to call the *InitializeSecurity* method to enable security features, such as message signing."

Example: Fabrikam Phone 1.0

Table 4-7 shows two external security notes for the Fabrikam Phone 1.0 application; these notes inform the user about actions that are necessary to maintain a secure configuration. The first example documents the fact that a default numeric password exists for the remote administration interface. The user will likely want to change this password so that an adversary trying to guess it has a more difficult time. The second example points out that local access control must be enabled to restrict outbound calling. In its default configuration, the phone does not restrict who can make outgoing calls.

Table 4-7   External Security Notes: Fabrikam Phone 1.0

ID	Description
1	Phone 1.0 has a remote administration interface with a default numeric password. Although the interface is disabled by default, the end user should ensure that the password is changed if the feature is enabled.
4	If the end user wants to control who can make outgoing calls, local access control should be enabled.

Example: Humongous Insurance Price Quote Website

Table 4-8 shows an external security note from the Humongous Insurance Price Quote Website; it informs the user that the website does not manage password quality. In other words, a user can utilize any password she wants, including a single character. Therefore, the user must create a strong password that is difficult to guess; otherwise, she runs the risk of an adversary accessing her account.

Table 4-8   External Security Notes: Humongous Insurance Price Quote Website

ID	Description
1	The website does not enforce password quality. Users and agents must choose strong passwords that are hard to guess or discover through brute force.

Example: A. Datum Access Control API

Table 4-9 shows an external security note from the A. Datum Access Control API; it documents behavior that is considered correct as far as the architects of the library are concerned, but this information could be misused by the end user. The user is informed so that he does not misinterpret how the library behaves under these circumstances.

Table 4-9   External Security Notes: A. Datum Access Control API

ID	Description
3	Requesting access to a resource with no flags set (*FlagRead = 1, FlagWrite = 2, FlagReadWrite = 3*) will always return access granted. Because no access rights were requested, this is considered correct behavior. However, calling applications should be aware of this case and ensure that they use it appropriately.

Internal Security Notes

Internal security notes contain information that readers of the threat model document should be aware of so that the model is clearer. These notes are used to explain trade-offs made in the design or implementation of the system that affect security, but they should not be used as a replacement for documentation of threats and vulnerabilities. Typically, internal security notes describe choices made for a business reason, backward compatibility, or another function impacting the system's security.

In the office building scenario, an example of an internal security note is that a card-key access system tying a specific employee in the human resources (HR) computer system to a card key is more expensive than a system that functions independently of the HR system. Therefore, an employee who is let go might become a threat by trying to access the building after his termination. Because card-key termination is not automated when the employee is removed from the HR database, it is possible that a malicious ex-employee might still have card-key access to building.

> **Caution**   Internal security notes should be used sparingly. They should document obvious security issues that cannot be mitigated because of an overriding nonsecurity need. They should not contain information that is not directly related to such an issue.

Relevance to the Threat Model

■   **Who uses the information?**   Internal security notes are used by reviewers of the threat model to understand security trade-offs that were made in the system design or implementation process.

- **How is the information collected?**   Internal security notes are usually collected when the system is being modeled or when threats are being investigated. Often internal security notes arise when a threat exists because of a particular design decision made to satisfy other, nonsecurity requirements.

- **How is this information used in the rest of the threat model?**   Internal security notes are used when the threat model is reviewed for completeness. They are also used when mitigation for vulnerabilities is discussed.

Data to Collect

When gathering internal security notes for the threat model document, the development team must collect the following details:

- **Numerical ID**   A unique number should be assigned to the internal security note. This can be referenced during threat investigation to discuss situations in which mitigation might not be possible.

- **Description**   A description of the security trade-off that was made should be recorded. Justification for that decision is also important. For example: "Message encryption was not implemented in the system because the engineering time would have caused the ship date for the product to slip."

Example: Fabrikam Phone 1.0

Table 4-10 shows an internal security note for the Fabrikam Phone 1.0 application; it describes the trade-off between manufacturing the phone using a battery backup with volatile RAM and doing so using nonvolatile RAM. Although the latter is cheaper to manufacture, it introduces denial-of-service threats.

Table 4-10   Internal Security Notes: Fabrikam Phone 1.0

ID	Description
1	Speed-dial information, messages, and the outgoing message are all stored in volatile RAM. The combination of volatile RAM and a battery backup for Phone 1.0 is cheaper to manufacture than using nonvolatile RAM. However, this means power loss to Phone 1.0 can cause loss of information if the battery backup is depleted.

Example: Humongous Insurance Price Quote Website

Table 4-11 shows an internal security note from the Humongous Insurance Price Quote Website; it points out that integrated authentication is not used.

Therefore, end-to-end authentication through delegation is not possible. Manual reauthentication using SQL authentication would take time and require extra administration. Furthermore, using anything but a single account for connections to the SQL server would preclude the use of connection pooling, causing a performance drop. Because of this, the website must store credentials for an account used to communicate with the SQL server. In addition, row-level access control is not possible because all queries to the SQL server are performed by using the same identity.

Table 4-11   Internal Security Notes: Humongous Insurance Price Quote Website

ID	Description
1	Because the website does not use integrated authentication of any kind, end-to-end authentication and identity are not used. Supporting SQL authentication would delay the deployment of the website. In addition, the database in use supports connection pooling only when all connections use the same credentials. Thus, all queries to the database are done by using one set of credentials (namely, the process identity of the Web server). Thus, if an attack such as SQL injection were to occur, the adversary would have access to all tables in the database.

Example: A. Datum Access Control API

Table 4-12 shows an internal security note for the A. Datum Access Control API; it describes a trade-off between memory and CPU resources. When explicit mode is enabled, only paths existing in the resource tree are checked. If explicit mode is disabled for the A. Datum Access Control API, the library creates resource nodes transparently, inheriting the permissions of their parent nodes. However, the library does not cache these nodes. Not caching the nodes mitigates an attack in which an adversary tries to exhaust memory resources by requesting implicitly generated notes. But this mitigation comes at the cost of re-creating implicit nodes each time one is requested, expending extra CPU cycles.

Table 4-12   Internal Security Notes: A. Datum Access Control API

ID	Description
1	To prevent a user from causing a denial of service by repeatedly requesting resources that do not exist when Explicit mode is disabled, the implicitly generated resource nodes are not stored in the *ACResources* tree. Rather, they are created and returned to the caller who is expected to free the *ACResource* instance after using it. This helps mitigate an out-of-memory condition but requires re-creating implicit nodes on each request.

Implementation Assumptions

Starting the threat modeling process before a system is implemented is beneficial. A majority of the threat model process, up to and including identifying threats, can be performed with only the system's design. However, once the system is implemented, it can add data points to each step of the process. Therefore, the development team should revisit the threat model to add this information.

Implementation assumptions are used when some or all of the system is in the design phase. These assumptions dictate specifics about features of the system that have yet to be implemented. These details must be true for the system to remain secure. During design analysis, potential vulnerabilities pending implementation are often identified. Identifying these vulnerabilities in the implementation assumptions allows them to be mitigated when coding occurs.

For example, the inside of the office building might require full floor-to-ceiling walls. In some areas, walls that extend only as high as the drop ceiling are common so that the office can be reconfigured without disturbing the ceiling or the services hidden by it, such as ventilation. However, this leaves a gap above the ceiling tiles that an adversary could use to gain access to locked rooms. Thus, it is critical that an office building requiring additional security note in its implementation assumptions that the walls should be built as full walls.

> **Note** Implementation assumptions should be validated on completion of the project. Plus, the threat model as a whole should be revised to reflect the implementation. Implementation assumptions that are not adhered to will often result in vulnerabilities.

Relevance to the Threat Model

- **Who uses the information?** The information is used by the developer of the relevant feature in the system. An implementation assumption is essentially a coding guideline that the developer must adhere to. After implementation, the threat model team should validate that the implementation assumption holds true. Implementation assumptions can also be validated in code reviews and during penetration testing.

■ **How is the information collected?**   When threats are identified, they often include threats that are common globally or to the team responsible for the system. If the threat is best mitigated during implementation rather than during design, the team usually has a common method of mitigating that threat in code. Thus, implementation assumptions are simply notes for the developer that include this information.

■ **How is this information used in the rest of the threat model?**   Implementation assumptions are invalidation points for the threat model if they do not remain true after the functionality is implemented. In addition, they are used as discussion points while revising a threat model started during the design phase.

Data to Collect

Development teams preparing a system's threat modeling document should collect the following details on the model's implementation assumptions:

■ **Numerical ID**   A unique number should be assigned to the implementation assumption for reference.

■ **Description**   The description should explain the method of implementation—for example: "Access control should be applied to the temporary file so that it matches the access granted to the source of the original data file."

Example: Fabrikam Phone 1.0

Table 4-13 shows implementation assumptions for the Fabrikam Phone 1.0 application; this table documents issues around secure communications. Fabrikam Phone 1.0's voice dialing capability has not been added to the phone. The first sample implementation assumption ensures that when the feature is implemented, it takes into account the existing access control. For example, a user should not be able to lift the handset and say, "Call Bob," without entering the access control passcode.

The second sample mentions that an encrypted communication feature might be added to the phone in the future. This feature would presumably allow two users to have a secure conversation over the PSTN, which was previously mentioned as potentially hostile. If this feature is added, it is essential that industry-accepted cryptography standards are applied.

Table 4-13   Implementation Assumptions: Fabrikam Phone 1.0

ID	Description
1	The voice-command dialing option has yet to be implemented. When this option is added, it should not introduce a way for adversaries to bypass current security features, such as long-distance call lockout.
2	If encrypted communication is added, key exchange should be done according to industry-accepted standards.

Example: Humongous Insurance Price Quote Website

Table 4-14 shows an implementation assumption for the Humongous Insurance Price Quote Website; it documents that the Price Quote Website has been fully implemented. Thus, no implementation assumptions exist. Including this documentation demonstrates that implementation assumptions were considered and removes any doubt that they were overlooked during the threat modeling process. If implementation assumptions in a threat model are later added to the system and verified as correct, it is best to leave them in the threat model and simply mark them as verified.

Table 4-14   Implementation Assumptions: Humongous Insurance Price Quote Website

ID	Description
1	None. The Price Quote Website is fully implemented.

Example: A. Datum Access Control API

Table 4-15 shows an implementation assumption from the A. Datum Access Control API; it describes the following security-critical implementation note: Deny access control entries should have precedence. A mistake here would change the access control semantics adversely.

Table 4-15   Implementation Assumption: A. Datum Access Control API

ID	Description
1	If Deny is added to the Access Control API, any Deny permission should have precedence over any Allow permission. Therefore, if a user is denied access to a resource or that user belongs to a group that is denied access, that determination has precedence over any Allow granted to the user or a group he belongs to.

Modeling the Application Through Data Flow Diagrams

Data flow diagrams (DFDs) are used in threat modeling to better understand the operation of a system. They provide a visual representation of how the system processes data. This allows the system to be modeled by focusing on transformations and processes applied to data and requests an adversary might supply. DFDs are also used later in the threat modeling process when the document is reviewed or used by security testers.

> **Note**   Exclusive use of DFDs in a threat model is not necessary. Some systems are better modeled using other standards, such as UML or flow charts. The important part of this stage of threat modeling is to create a better understanding of how the system works and how its subsystems fit together; the type of diagramming system used is less important. However, DFDs are the primary method for modeling the system recommended by this process.

One advantage of using DFDs is that they are hierarchical in nature. In addition, not all areas of the system need to be modeled to the same detail, as this section will demonstrate. Thus, modelers need focus on only security-critical components.

When creating DFDs or other system models, weigh the time spent creating the diagrams against the benefit of doing so. DFDs should not be created simply for the sake of placing them in the document. A simple rule of thumb is to always create an overall context diagram and to create lower-level diagrams for anything that is important enough to be sketched on the whiteboard or other presentation device used during the threat modeling meetings. In other words, any visual aid created during the threat modeling discussions should be captured in the threat modeling document.

Concepts

Data flow diagramming focuses on data as it moves through the system and the transforms that are applied to that data. Six basic shapes are used in DFDs for threat modeling: process, multiple process, external entity, data store, data flow, and privilege boundary.

Process

The process shape, shown in Figure 4-5, represents a task in the system that processes data or performs some action based on the data. Descriptions should be succinct, outlining the process that is performed in terms of an action. Process nodes should be numbered as described in the figure.

Figure 4-5   Process element.

Multiple Process

The multiple process shape, shown in Figure 4-6, is made up of subprocesses. The multiple process element should be used whenever the process is further broken down in a lower-level DFD. Multiple process elements should be numbered and described.

Figure 4-6   Multiple process element.

When a process or multiple process node is a subnode of a node in another diagram, the numbering is prefixed by the number of the parent node. Thus, if node C is a child of node B, which is a child of node A, the numbering might look like this:

Node	Number
A	1
B	1.2
C	1.2.1

External Entity

The external entity shape (shown in Figure 4-7) represents an interactor that exists outside the system being modeled and which interacts with the system at an entry point. External entities are either the source or destination of data, and they can interact only with processes or multiple processes.

> **Note**   Two external entities or an external entity and a data flow communicating with each other are considered irrelevant to the DFD and the threat model because they represent two external systems communicating. Thus, they are inherently outside the system being modeled. (Data flows, which represent data being transferred between other elements, are discussed in more detail later in the section.)

Figure 4-7   External entity element.

Data Store

The data store shape (shown in Figure 4-8) represents a repository for data—such as the registry, file system, or database—where data is saved or retrieved. Data stores do not change they data they contain. As with external entities, data stores can interact only with single or multiple processes.

Figure 4-8   Data store element.

Data Flow

The data flow shape (shown in Figure 4-9) represents data being transferred between other elements. The direction of the flow is indicated with an arrow. Each data flow represents a logical set of data, such as a data structure, byte stream, string of text, and so on. Data flows should be labeled with descriptive text.

Data Flow

Figure 4-9   Data flow element.

Privilege Boundary

The privilege boundary shape (shown in Figure 4-10) is a shape specific to threat modeling and not found in traditional DFDs. This shape represents a boundary between nodes that have different privilege levels. The privilege boundary can describe locations where

■   A privilege impersonation on the part of an adversary could occur.

■   A security assertion in managed code could occur.

■   A machine or process boundary may be crossed.

■   The privileges between nodes may differ.

/ Privilege Boundary

Figure 4-10   Privilege boundary element.

DFD Hierarchy

As mentioned, DFDs are iterative, organized in a hierarchy. Processing nodes that need to be further described are expanded in lower-level diagrams. Not all processes need to be expanded to the same level; only processes that would benefit from a more detailed visual explanation need to be expanded. As lower-level diagrams are created (from context, to Level 0, to Level 1, and so on), the processing nodes and data in the data flows become more specific. Furthermore, a lower-level diagram represents a detailed view of a single processing node in a higher diagram. Therefore, a system with three processing nodes in its Level 0 diagram will have at most three Level 1 diagrams, one showing detailed processing for each of the higher-level processing nodes in the Level 0 diagram.

As shown in Figure 4-11, the *context diagram* is the root diagram in a set of DFDs. This diagram represents the entire system as a single process node. External entities and data stores interface with the process node via data flows.

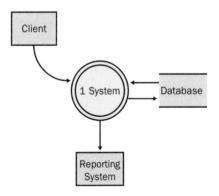

Figure 4-11   Context diagram.

Lower-level diagrams, such as those shown in Figure 4-12 and Figure 4-13, expand a multiple process node into more multiple process nodes. When numbering process nodes, order is not important—the numeric labels are simply indexes.

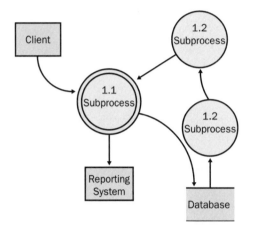

Figure 4-12   Level 0 diagram.

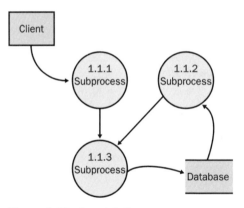

Figure 4-13   Level 1 diagram.

Using DFDs in Threat Modeling

When used in threat modeling, DFDs can accurately reflect the adversary's view of the system. At the context-diagram level, the system as a whole is represented as a single process node. External entities and data stores interact with the system via data flows. This follows the notion that any intersection between a data flow originating or terminating at an external entity and the system's context-level process node is actually an entry point. In a complete context diagram, all entry points will be represented by such an intersection.

In the presentation of the office building example in Chapter 3, several entry points were discussed. Figure 4-14 shows a context diagram for the entire office building.

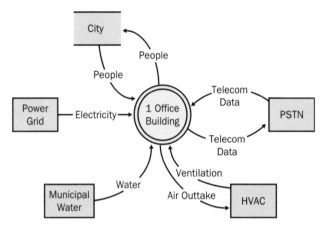

Figure 4-14   Context diagram for an office building.

> **Note**   Data flows are not always symmetric. For example, in the office building diagram in Figure 4-14, electricity from the power grid flows in, but nothing flows back out. It could be argued that the electric bill is an outward data flow; however, the bill goes to the power company, not the power grid.

Numbering Diagrams

Lower-level data flow diagrams are used to model the processing into the system that occurs at each entry point. Although the entire functionality of the system is represented as a single process node in the context diagram, that functionality is broken into multiple process nodes in a Level 0 diagram. From there, a Level 1 diagram, a Level 2 diagram, and so on can be constructed to more precisely model security-critical processing. Using an appropriate numbering scheme as described earlier in the section can help better organize DFDs.

Including Privilege Boundaries

Threat modeling DFDs should be extended to include privilege boundaries, which can help identify threats. Privilege boundaries, represented with a dashed line, separate two processing nodes (or a processing node and an external entity or data store) that have different trust levels associated with them or that perform actions requiring different trust levels.

In the office building example, a privilege boundary exists at the external door. This is the card-key access system described earlier in the chapter. The DFD in Figure 4-15 shows this boundary. Nodes on one side of the boundary have a lower privilege level than nodes on the other side. On the left side (nodes 1.1.1 and 1.1.3), the privilege level is anonymous because the system has made no determination as to the person's identity. On the right side (nodes 1.1.2 and 1.1.4), processing occurs at a higher privilege level, because the person's identity has been established and trusted operations (such as unlocking the door) can then occur.

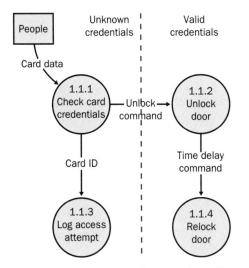

Figure 4-15   A Level 1 diagram of an office building depicting process at the front door and a privilege boundary.

Relevance to the Threat Model

DFDs are the preferred method of diagramming the system in threat modeling because they show processes that occur based on data input. As mentioned earlier, an adversary cannot attack a software system without supplying it with data. Therefore, threats to a system can occur anywhere the system transforms, takes action based on, or otherwise processes data that is ultimately supplied by the adversary. Thus, threats occur at process nodes. The *threat path* is defined as the sequence of any process nodes that perform security-critical processing—that is, any of the aforementioned nodes that process data or requests from a potentially malicious source. Knowing what data is supplied to the node allows a development team to understand how an adversary can attack that node. Knowing what that node does allows the team to understand the damage a successful attack could cause. Nodes on the threat path require particular scrutiny.

- **Who uses the information?**   DFDs are used by the threat modeling team to better understand the system. DFDs can also be used by security testers to better understand the system's functionality and implementation. The visual representation of the data flows allows the tester to create attack hypotheses.

- **How is the information collected?**   The architects and developers of the system provide this information. DFDs are often partially completed before any threat modeling meetings occur. During the meetings, however, DFDs are usually expanded, with more diagrams being created as the team analyzes the system.

- **How is this information used in the rest of the threat model?**   The DFDs are used during threat identification as a way to direct threat hypotheses. These diagrams allow the threat modeling team to better understand the functionality exposed by the system and an attacker's possible goals.

Example: Fabrikam Phone 1.0

Figure 4-16 is a Level 1 DFD for the Fabrikam Phone 1.0 application.

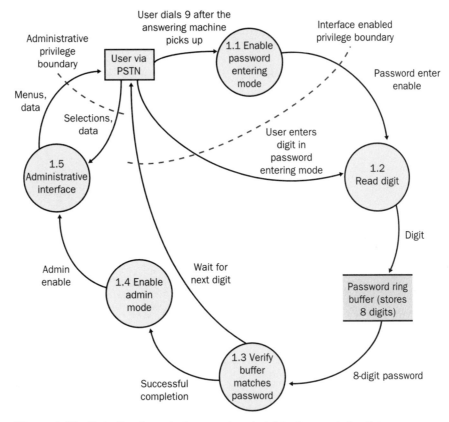

Figure 4-16   Data flow for entering remote administrative mode for Fabrikam Phone 1.0.

The DFD in the figure shows the data flow for entering remote administrative mode on the phone system. This DFD shows how the password ring buffer is used to determine whether the correct password has been entered.

Note , This example is the basis for a hypothetical threat discussed in Chapter 5.

Example: Humongous Insurance Price Quote Website

Figure 4-17 is the context diagram for the Humongous Insurance Price Quote Website.

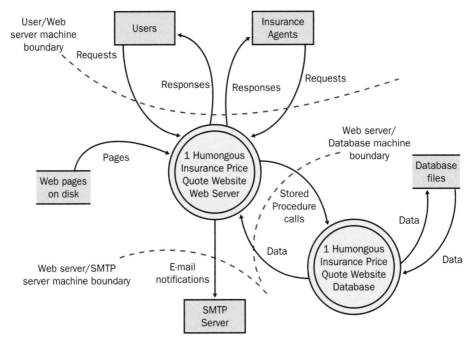

Figure 4-17   Context diagram for the Humongous InsurancePrice Quote Website.

Machine boundaries appear as privilege boundaries in this figure. This context diagram is incorrect from a purist standpoint because it does not represent the entire system as a single multiple-process node. The single multiple-process node typically shown in a context diagram is split into two processing nodes to illustrate that the website exists across several machines. In general, doing this is advised only in situations when necessary to best illustrate the system model.

Example: A. Datum Access Control API

Figure 4-18 is a Level 2 diagram for the the A. Datum Access Control API.

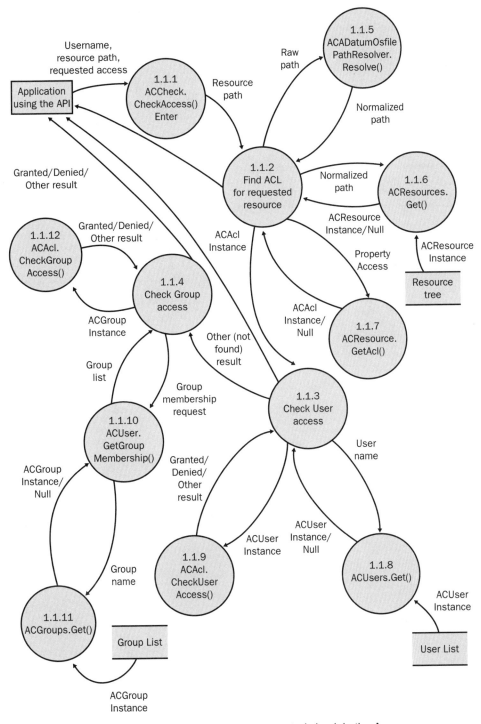

Figure 4-18   Level 2 diagram showing an access control check in the A. Datum Access Control API.

This figure shows the current implementation of the access control check used in the threat model analysis. This diagram is the basis for a vulnerability discussed in Chapter 5, where a user is a member of a group that is denied access to a resource, but that user has an Allow access control entry. In the DFD, if the user check succeeds, the user is granted access. However, because Deny access control entries should be applied before Allow access control entries, the user should be denied based on her group membership.

Summary

Before enumerating and analyzing threats, the development team must understand the system being modeled. This is a two-stage process, consisting of collecting background information to scope the threat discussion and modeling the functionality of the system through data flow diagrams, or DFDs.

This phase in the threat modeling process is necessary to constrain the threat model discussion, understand external dependencies, and collect security-critical information for users, reviewers, and developers. In addition, this phase enables development teams to further understand the functionality of the system with regard to processing input data.

5

The Threat Profile

The threat profile of a system outlines the possible goals of an adversary and the system's susceptibility to those goals, or vulnerabilities. The threat modeling document describes a system's threat profile to quantify the security of the system. The enumeration of possible adversary goals must be complete; the weaknesses of the system that will be identified through threat modeling are a subset of these threats.

The threat profile is best examined in terms of a design specification for the security of the system. Each threat in the profile must be prevented or mitigated, either by the design or the implementation of the system. These threats will also drive system security features. In other words, each security feature should correspond to a threat that it has been designed to counter.

Threats to the system must be analyzed to determine whether any vulnerabilities exist. Threats not sufficiently mitigated are considered vulnerabilities. This investigation can be done by using threat trees, analytical tools describing a particular threat's attack paths. Threat trees allow each threat's implications to be considered with regard to the system design and implementation.

This chapter covers the following steps of creating a threat profile:

- Identifying threats to the system
- Investigating threats by using threat trees
- Resolving or mitigating vulnerabilities

Identifying Threats

A threat to a system will not go away, assuming the functionality and asset the threat targets remain part of the system. To prevent the threat from turning into a vulnerability, mitigation must occur. Identifying threats is key to developing a robust system. This step is often the most difficult part of threat modeling. However, with the collected entry points and assets, the proper gathering of background information on the system, and the creation of data flow diagrams (DFDs)—discussed in Chapters 3 and 4—identifying threats can be straightforward.

The threat modeling team must use the information gathered so far to create attack hypotheses. To identify threats, the threat modeling team asks itself this question about each entry point: "What security-critical processing occurs, and what might a malicious external entity do to attack that processing or otherwise use an asset for some purpose other than its intended use?"

> **Note**   Do not confuse threats with vulnerabilities. A *threat* is simply a goal an adversary might *try* to achieve to abuse an asset in the system. A *vulnerability* is a specific way that a threat can be exploited through an unmitigated attack path. To create an accurate threat profile, threats with mitigated attack paths must still be identified. This fosters the characterization of how well the system enforces security.

Correlating Threats and Assets

Assets and threats have a close correlation. A threat cannot exist without a target asset. For a risk to exist, the system must possess something the adversary finds valuable. Threats are cross-referenced with assets in the threat model document to show this relationship. Furthermore, threats are typically prevented by applying some sort of protection to assets.

Threats represent either the misuse of or damage to an asset existing outside normal system operations. In the office building example used throughout this book, threats correspond to the assets outlined in Chapter 3. One threat might be the disclosure of corporate data stored on the office's computer systems. Another threat might be the intrusion of unauthorized people into the office workspace, which could jeopardize the safety of employees. Figure 5-1 illustrates one of these threats to the office building.

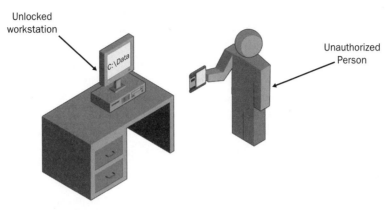

Figure 5-1   Possible threats to an office building.

Creating Adversary Hypotheses

The process of correlating threats to an asset involves creating adversary hypotheses. Just as designing a system means specifying how it should operate and be used, threat modeling a system means specifying how an adversary could make the system fail or abuse it. Understanding what an adversary stands to gain from an asset is key to outlining these hypotheses.

Starting with a Known Vulnerability

As an example, consider the buffer overflow, a classic implementation vulnerability. A buffer overflow affects the integrity of the application's process space. Because the bounds of a buffer have been exceeded, contiguous data can no longer be trusted. Threat modeling to find the buffer overflow requires that an asset be identified (process integrity) and a corresponding threat be hypothesized. For instance, a threat to a Web server might be an adversary sending a malformed URL in a *GET* request, in an attempt to compromise the server's process integrity.

> **More Info**   Investigating attack vectors for this type of threat will be discussed later in the chapter in the "Investigating Threats with Threat Trees" section.

The threat against process integrity can enable the adversary to access several assets, each with a different level of severity. Suppose one vulnerability associated with the threat is a buffer overflow when the URL is sufficiently long. In this case, overwriting the contiguous data might cause the process to crash, resulting in a denial of service. However, the contiguous data in the process space could contain control-flow information, such as a saved program counter. In this case, data supplied by the adversary could cause arbitrary code of his choosing to execute, resulting in an elevation of privilege. Knowing what an adversary stands to gain by using a buffer overflow to manipulate the process integrity can help predict threats accurately.

This example started with a well-known vulnerability class and worked back to the root asset and threat. Collecting a list of vulnerabilities found in earlier versions of the application as well as in similar applications produced by other companies can help the threat modeling team determine the root assets and threats to it.

> **Tip**   Starting with a known vulnerability is one way of determining threats to a system when the threat modeling team is new to the process.

This approach does have its limitations, however. Every system is unique, and although two systems might share assets and threats, a certain amount of their assets and threats will be system specific. Thus, portions of their threat profiles will differ. Although working backward from past vulnerabilities typically yields common threats, system-specific threats require deeper analysis of the unique qualities of the application being modeled.

Using known vulnerabilities as a starting point helps feed the rest of the threat model. By identifying root assets and threats, the threat modeling team can hypothesize about variations on known issues. Furthermore, in determining this information, the team can better understand and accurately model the underlying motivations of the adversary.

Starting with the System's Assets

When starting with known vulnerabilities, teams tend to confuse threats with vulnerabilities, which can devalue the threat profile. A better method of threat enumeration is to step through each of the system's assets, reviewing a list of high-level attack goals for each asset. For starters, the threat model team can ask the following questions:

- How could the adversary use or manipulate the asset to
  - ❏ Modify the control flow of the system?
  - ❏ Retrieve information that should be restricted?
  - ❏ Manipulate information within the system?
  - ❏ Cause the system to fail or become unusable?
  - ❏ Gain additional rights?
- Can the adversary access the asset
  - ❏ Without being audited?
  - ❏ And skip any access control checks?
  - ❏ And appear to be another user?

Important Such high-level categorical questions can help drive the threat modeling conversation. But these questions can be limiting, too, prompting threat modeling teams to adopt a checklist mentality. Teams should also note that the questions asked will change from asset to asset and system to system.

For instance, in examining the asset of network connectivity—that is, the ability of nodes to communicate with each other—for a peer-to-peer networking application, a threat modeling team might detect various threats against this asset that an adversary could exploit to render the system unusable.

Threats cannot simply be identified. Each threat must be analyzed to determine whether the system is susceptible to it, resulting in a vulnerability. The threat modeling team must determine whether the system appropriately mitigates against each threat. The preferred method of investigating threats is to use analytical tools known as *threat trees* (discussed in more detail in the next section). Threat trees are derived from fault trees and draw from Edward G. Amoroso's work in *Fundamentals of Computer Security Technology* (Pearson, 1994). Some threats, particularly those targeting implementation issues, are analyzed by using code reviews and penetration testing. Regardless of the method used to investigate threats, it is critical the threat modeling team perform this step.

Classifying Threat Effects Through STRIDE

Once threats are identified, they should be categorized. The model commonly used for this is STRIDE, documented in *Writing Secure Code, Second Edition* (Microsoft Press, 2003), by Michael Howard and David LeBlanc. STRIDE is a classification of the effects of realizing a threat: Spoofing, Tampering, Repudiation, Information disclosure, Denial of service, and Elevation of privilege.

- **Spoofing**   Allows an adversary to pose as another user, component, or other system that has an identity in the system being modeled.

- **Tampering**   The modification of data within the system to achieve a malicious goal.

- **Repudiation**   The ability of an adversary to deny performing some malicious activity because the system does not have sufficient evidence to prove otherwise.

- **Information disclosure**   The exposure of protected data to a user that is not otherwise allowed access to that data.

- **Denial of service**   Occurs when an adversary can prevent legitimate users from using the normal functionality of the system.

- **Elevation of privilege**   Occurs when an adversary uses illegitimate means to assume a trust level with different privileges than he currently has.

A high-level classification of the threat makes it easier to understand what that threat allows an attacker to do. Furthermore, it helps assign priority to threats. In most systems, elevation of privilege threats carry the most risk because they would allow an attacker to perform functionality normally restricted to another user. However, in other systems, repudiation might be just as critical (such as in a financial system where failure to properly audit actions could have legal and monetary implications).

Threats often fit into multiple categories of the STRIDE model. Development teams need to understand the underlying effect a threat has on the system when classifying threats with the STRIDE model. For example, some threats are purely of the tampering nature; others might enable tampering but arise as a result of elevation of privilege. Developers must ensure they understand the root effect; otherwise, they might not classify the threat correctly.

Relevance to the Threat Model

■ **Who uses the information?**   Managers use threat information to determine the security strengths of the system they are responsible for. Security testers use threat data and their associated threat trees to test how resilient the system is to attacks.

■ **How is the information collected?**   People responsible for the system's implementation and design are good sources of threat information. In addition, it is a good idea to consult with people who did not work on the system during the threat modeling process. These individuals often can think more critically about the system because they are not biased by having worked on it.

■ **How is this information used in the rest of the threat model?**   Threats are later analyzed to determine whether any vulnerabilities are associated with them. Threats are the basis for determining the strengths and weaknesses of the system. Threats also provide the basis for a secure system design.

Data to Collect

When compiling an application's threat model, the modeling team must gather the following information about the threats they want to protect the system against:

■ **Numerical ID**   A unique number should be assigned to the threat for reference.

■ **Name**   This is a short title for the threat and should be descriptive enough to identify the threat as well as the target asset. An example of this is, "The adversary views another user's personal information."

■ **Description**   The description should provide additional details about the nature of the threat.

■ **STRIDE classification**   The STRIDE model is used to help understand the effect of realizing a specific threat. For more on STRIDE, see the "Classifying Threat Effects Through STRIDE" sidebar.

■ **Corresponding entry points**   The entry points that the threat applies to should be cross-referenced so that the threats can use this information for prioritization.

■ **Relevant assets**   Assets that the threat applies to are also listed because a threat must always have a target asset.

■ **Mitigation**   All threats must be investigated to determine whether the threat is mitigated. This information must be recorded in the threat model document.

Example: Fabrikam Phone 1.0

Table 5-1 shows a phone configuration threat to Fabrikam's Phone 1.0 application. This threat describes the attack goal of gaining access to the remote administration interface. One method of mitigating this threat is to use passwords. Note, however, that the threat cross-references an external security note as part of its mitigation. If the default password is not changed, a system vulnerability will develop. This can be mitigated by informing the user to change the default password. Note that cross-references to other information, such as entry points, show the corresponding numerical ID in parentheses.

Table 5-1   Fabrikam Phone 1.0 Phone Configuration Threat

ID	1
Name	An adversary gains access to the remote administration interface, resulting in access to the phone configuration.
Description	Phone 1.0 has a remote administration interface that allows an authorized user to configure it via the Public Switched Telephone Network (PSTN). The interface is disabled by default but can be enabled using the local keypad.
STRIDE classification	■ Tampering ■ Information disclosure ■ Denial of service ■ Elevation of privilege
Mitigated?	No
Known mitigation	If the remote administration interface is enabled, the end user should change the default password. *Related external security note:* (1) Phone 1.0 has a remote administration interface with a default numeric password. Although the interface is disabled by default, the end user should ensure that the password is changed if the feature is enabled.
Entry points	(6) Remote administration (3) Telephone line (2) Keypad
Assets	(5) Phone configuration

As another example, Table 5-2 shows the threat of an adversary making a long-distance call using Fabrikam's Phone 1.0. This threat is relatively straightforward. It can be traced directly to a monetary value because long-distance calling usually involves an additional charge beyond basic phone service. As with an adversary accessing the remote administration interface, this threat is primarily mitigated through the use of passwords.

Table 5-2   Fabrikam Phone 1.0 Long-Distance Calling Threat

ID	3
Name	An adversary makes a long-distance call.
Description	Access to long-distance phone service can be restricted. Often it is not desirable for arbitrary users to make long-distance calls.
STRIDE classification	Elevation of privilege
Mitigated?	Yes
Known mitigation	If the local access control is disabled, this threat cannot be protected against. If the control is enabled, brute force attacking the password would be difficult because the phone requires eight-digit passwords and the passwords are entered via the keypad. If the password is disclosed by the phone's owner, it is not the responsibility of Phone 1.0.
	If a long-distance password has not been configured and the local access control is enabled, the phone defaults to the local access control password for long distance. The local access control must be enabled for the long-distance password to be configured. The long-distance password will also grant the same rights that the local call password does.
	Related use scenarios:
	(2) If the Phone 1.0 is installed in a location where untrusted users can access it, it should have local access control enabled.
	Related external security notes:
	(3) The long-distance password can be enabled only when local access control is enabled. Further, entering the long-distance password allows local calls to be made.
Entry points	(1) Handset
	(2) Keypad
Assets	(4) Long-distance calling

Example: Humongous Insurance Price Quote Website

Tables 5-3 shows a threat to the backend database for the Humongous Insurance Price Quote Website. Many software systems take input that is reparsed at some point during the processing. Such parsing often relies on special characters, escape codes, keywords, or similar entities to decode the request. A common threat for these systems is an adversary supplying malformed input. Such an attack can include injecting this special data into the user's input in an attempt to force the system to parse the data differently than the programmer intended. SQL injection is an example of a vulnerability associated with this type of threat, and it can enable additional SQL commands to be executed or the original command's behavior to be modified.

> **Note** This is an implementation threat—a threat that is best mitigated through secure coding practices—and so it is best investigated through code review or penetration testing.

Table 5-3 Humongous Insurance Price Quote Website Database Threat

ID	1
Name	An adversary supplies malicious data in a request targeting the SQL command parsing engine in an attempt to change execution.
Description	An adversary might try to insert SQL commands or special characters into the data she supplies, such as her login name or personal information. If this data is not handled properly by the Price Quote Website, it could result in a SQL injection vulnerability. Other malicious input could cause the system to become unstable or leak information.
STRIDE classification	■ Tampering ■ Elevation of privilege
Mitigated?	No
Known mitigation	Not mitigated. See corresponding vulnerability ID #1.
Entry points	(1.1) Login page (1.2) Data entry page (1.3) Insurance agent quote review page
Assets	(16.3) Access to backend database

Tables 5-4 shows a threat to the user login data of the Humongous Insurance Price Quote Website. For Web applications that maintain user accounts, a typical threat is an adversary acquiring another user's credentials. This gives the adversary the full rights of the other user and is obviously not desirable.

Table 5-4   Humongous Insurance Price Quote Website Threat to Login Data

ID	2
Name	An adversary acquires the username and password of another user or insurance agent.
Description	If an adversary obtains another user's login credentials, he can do anything that person can on the website.
STRIDE classification	■ Information disclosure ■ Elevation of privilege
Mitigated?	No
Known mitigation	*Related use scenarios:* (3) The database server should be protected from direct access from the Internet by a firewall. *Related external security notes:* (1) The website does not enforce password quality. Users and agents must choose strong passwords that are hard to guess or discover through brute force.
Entry points	(1.1) Login page (2.1) Database stored procedures
Assets	(13.1) User's login data (13.7) Insurance agent's login data

Example: A. Datum Access Control API

Table 5-5 shows a code execution threat against the A. Datum Access Control API. Threats that target parsing code, which could result in vulnerabilities such as buffer overflows and integer overflows, should be considered when input data can be of a variable length. Despite having been a common threat in the development world for some time now (recall as mentioned in Chapter 1 that the Morris Internet worm exploited a buffer overflow 15 years ago), implementation issues still occur when parsing user input.

> **Caution**   Never assume that an adversary will provide expected input. Rather, the adversary will often stretch the limits of a protocol or specification, often finding a system's vulnerabilities. This is another example of a threat that is best investigated through code review and penetration testing.

Table 5-5   **A. Datum Access Control API Code Execution Threat**

ID	3
Name	An adversary supplies malicious or malformed data as a path to the library, targeting the path parsing the code.
Description	An attacker could use malicious input, such as long resource paths, in an attempt to overflow a character buffer or integer-length field.
STRIDE classification	Elevation of privilege
Mitigated?	No
Known mitigation	Not mitigated. See corresponding vulnerability IDs #1 and 2.
Entry points	(8) *IACPathResolver*
	(8.2) *ACADatumOSFilePathResolver*
	(1) *ACResources*
Assets	(8.6) Ability to execute arbitrary code as the identity of the process

Table 5-6 shows a path discovery threat against the A. Datum Access Control API. Not all threats result in elevation of privilege. An adversary detecting whether a specific path exists might seem innocuous, but the security of some systems depends on an adversary not knowing data paths, such as temporarily downloaded files. This is a good example of a threat that, if not mitigated, could be combined with other threats to create a more sophisticated attack.

Table 5-6   **A. Datum Access Control API Path Discovery Threat**

ID	9
Name	An adversary determines whether a specified path exists.
Description	The adversary might want to determine whether a specific path that he should not have access to exists. This might include determining whether the path exists in the resource tree or in the underlying system.
STRIDE classification	Information disclosure
Mitigated?	No
Known mitigation	This is partially mitigated because the Access Control API never interacts with the underlying system that stores the resources.
Entry points	(1) *ACResources*
Assets	(9.6) Path discovery

Investigating Threats with Threat Trees

Identifying threats is only part of creating the system's threat profile. Threats must also be analyzed to determine whether the system is susceptible to them. Using threat trees (sometimes called *attack trees*) is one way to accomplish this.

Analyzing with Threat Trees

Threat trees are used to determine whether the conditions necessary for a threat to be realized exist and are unmitigated. A threat tree consists of a *root node,* or threat, which has one or more *child conditions* that must be true for an adversary to realize the threat. Any child condition can in turn have one or more child conditions. Two or more conditions at the same level and sharing the same parent node can be combined, resulting in an AND relationship; otherwise, an implicit OR condition exists. Determining whether one or more vulnerabilities are associated with a threat is simply a matter of starting at a leaf condition (a node in the threat tree with no child nodes) and following it up to the root threat. If a path not broken by a mitigated node or a broken AND condition exists, a vulnerability exists.

When analyzing threats by using threat trees, the conditions in the tree have mitigation associated with them. This is because the conditions represent specific actions or situations that must occur, while the threat is less concrete. The conditions also have a risk associated with them, for which Microsoft often uses the DREAD rating system: Damage potential, Reproducibility, Exploitability, Affected users, and Discoverability.

Understanding Risk Through DREAD

The DREAD method of characterizing the risk associated with a vulnerability is documented in *Writing Secure Code, Second Edition* (Microsoft Press, 2003), by Michael Howard and David LeBlanc. The term *DREAD* stands for the following categories. When using the DREAD method, a threat modeling team calculates security risks as an average of numeric values assigned to each of these five categories.

- **Damage potential**   Ranks the extent of the damage that occurs if a vulnerability is exploited.

- **Reproducibility**   Ranks how often an attempt at exploiting a vulnerability works.

- **Exploitability**   Assigns a number to the effort required to exploit the vulnerability. In addition, exploitability considers preconditions such as whether the user must be authenticated.

- **Affected users**   A numeric value characterizing the ratio of installed instances of the system that would be affected if an exploit became widely available.

- **Discoverability**   Measures the likelihood that a vulnerability will be found by external security researchers, hackers, and the like if it went unpatched.

When using the DREAD method, be careful not to assign too wide a numerical range to the values. In most environments, a range of 1 to 3 is sufficient. Using a limited range allows a simplified definition of each rating, with straightforward examples. A limited range also makes categorizing the vulnerabilities less ambiguous and more meaningful. Consider the affected users rating; a range of three might correspond to:

1   Edge case—only users in nonstandard configurations for specific reasons

2   Common case—many users run in this configuration to support normal activity, but not the default configuration

3   Default case—all users unless they have specifically disabled the feature

This categorization is less vague than ten levels, for instance, which would be less discrete. Simplifying the range by using fewer, more meaningful values makes it easier for the team to assign a DREAD rating to a vulnerability. A range of ten in this example might correspond to percentages: 1 for 10%, 2 for 20%, and so on. But realistically, how meaningful is the difference between 60 percent of users and 70 percent of users? When it comes to rating risk, it is certainly better to use smaller ranges with values that are clearly defined by the threat modeling team up front.

Identifying Attack Paths

Threat trees are used in threat modeling to analyze how a threat might be accomplished through attack paths. An *attack path* is a route from a leaf condition to the root threat, inclusive of any AND condition. Threat trees are used to determine valid attack paths for a threat. And any attack path that does not have a mitigating node is classified as a vulnerability.

In its most basic form, a threat tree consists of a single threat and multiple AND conditions, mitigated conditions, and unmitigated conditions, as shown in Figure 5-2.

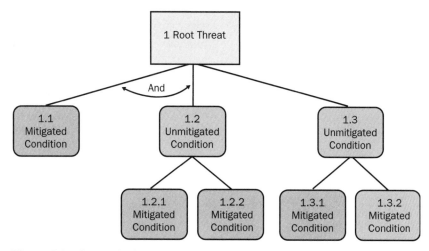

Figure 5-2   A sample threat tree.

The example in the figure shows four possible attack paths. Only one of these (the path from 1.3.2 to 1.3 to 1) has no mitigating nodes and thus represents a valid attack path or vulnerability.

Threat trees can be expressed graphically or as text in a threat modeling document. This threat tree in Figure 5-2 would look like this in textual representation:

```
1 Root Threat
    1.1 (and) (Mitigated) Mitigated Condition
    1.2 (and) Unmitigated Condition
        1.2.1 (Mitigated) Mitigated Condition
        1.2.2 (Mitigated) Mitigated Condition
    1.3 Unmitigated Condition
        1.3.1 (Mitigated) Mitigated Condition
        1.3.2 Unmitigated Condition
```

Figure 5-3 shows a threat tree for an adversary supplying a long URL to a Web server to compromise the server process integrity by exceeding a buffer allocation. In practice, threats that target implementation issues such as this are best analyzed through code reviews and penetration testing. This tree is partial; numerous other ways to cause an overflow could exist.

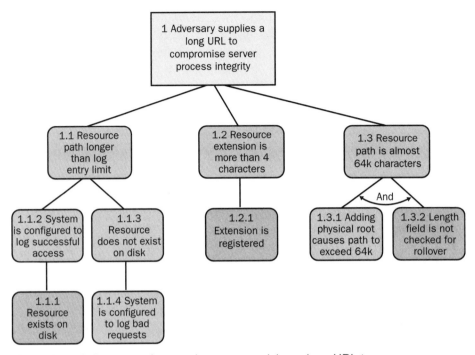

Figure 5-3 A threat tree for an adversary supplying a long URL to a Web server.

In addition to finding vulnerabilities associated with threats, threat trees can be useful for penetration testers who are creating simulated attacks against a system. Threat trees show logical steps for an attack against the system by using monatomic conditions that break down the test into individual tests.

Threat trees can also be combined. In other words, a threat tree can be collapsed and represented as a condition in another threat tree. This is called *attack chaining*. Attack chaining is useful for predicting more complex attacks as well as for creating application-level, scenario-based threat models (discussed in Chapter 6).

Relevance to the Threat Model

■ **Who uses the information?** Security testers use threat analysis information to construct tests to validate or challenge the system's security. Managers use the information to determine how well the system stands up to potential attacks.

- **How is the information collected?**   Threat modeling participants successively break down the threat into individual conditions and attack paths.

- **How is this information used in the rest of the threat model?**   This information is used to determine whether vulnerabilities exist for a given threat. If a threat tree has one or more valid attack paths, the threat is not properly mitigated, resulting in vulnerabilities.

Data to Collect

To investigate threats to a system and detect vulnerabilities, the threat modeling team should gather the following threat tree information:

- **Threat ID**   The ID of the corresponding threat should be cross-referenced.

- **Tree nodes**   The threat modeling team should record node data in the form of a graphic or textual representation of the tree. Diagramming utilities can be used to assist. Hierarchical data representations, such as XML, can also be used to store the threat trees.

Example: Fabrikam Phone 1.0

Figure 5-4 shows an example threat tree for Fabrikam Phone 1.0. The figure depicts possible routes through which an adversary could gain access to the remote administration interface. Threat trees can be constructed by answering the question, "What is required for this to occur?" in the parent-child relation and the question, "What else is needed or how else could this occur?" in the sibling relation.

For example, at node 1.1, the threat modeling team could ask, "How is the remote administration interface enabled?" The child node, 1.1.1, describes how this is done: "A local user enables the interface." Also, at node 1.1, the team could ask, "What else is needed if the remote administration interface is enabled?" Nodes 1.2 and 1.3 answer this, pointing out that the adversary must know and dial the phone number and obtain the password.

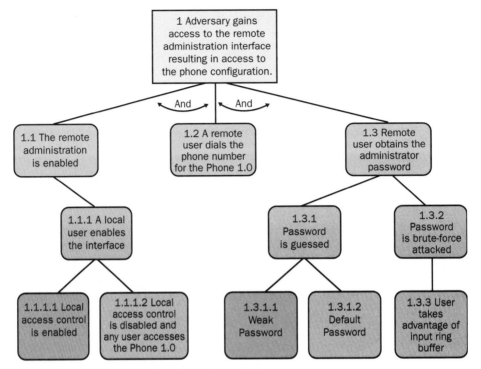

Figure 5-4   Threat tree for Fabrikam Phone 1.0.

Example: Humongous Insurance Price Quote Website

The threat tree shown in Figure 5-5 describes how an adversary might obtain another user's username and password. As with the example for Fabrikam Phone 1.0, the "how" relation is the parent-child one, and the "what or how else" relation is between the siblings. Constructing a threat tree in this manner prevents ambiguity and presents the threat breakdown logically.

Example: A. Datum Access Control API

Another method of constructing threat trees is to use them to compare and contrast conditions. Instead of using the "how" and "what or how else" questions, the threat tree will compare similar conditions at the sibling level. In the example in Figure 5-6, the first child level contrasts the difference between implicit and explicit resource node generation for the A. Datum Access Control API.

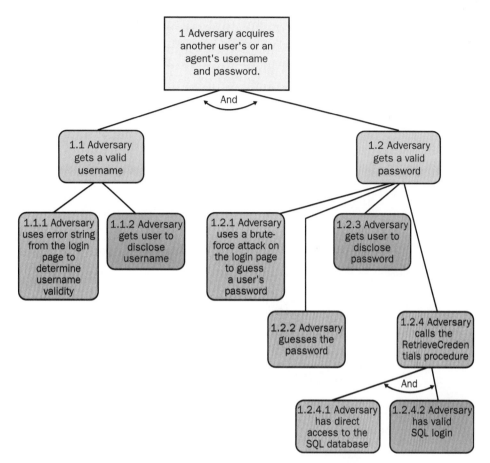

Figure 5-5   Threat tree for Humongous Insurance Price Quote Website.

When implicit mode is set, the attack path is immediately terminated by a mitigated condition. In explicit mode, it is possible to determine whether a node exists because the API will always return TRUE if it does or a not-found error if it does not. When building threat trees in this manner, leaf nodes are either mitigated conditions or the final condition that must be met to achieve the goal.

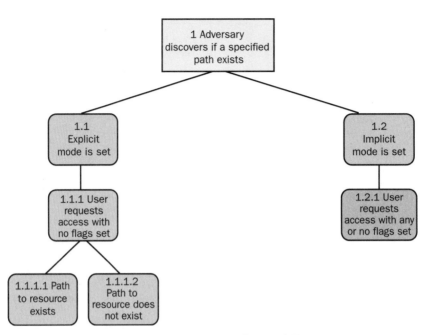

Figure 5-6 Threat tree for A. Datum Access Control API.

Vulnerability Resolution and Mitigation

Once vulnerabilities are found, they must be resolved or otherwise mitigated. Vulnerabilities are bugs—but with the added risk of having security implications. The threat model document includes vulnerabilities so that actions taken as a result of threat model discoveries are recorded. However, vulnerabilities, like other bugs, should be tracked using the development team bug-tracking database. If this database allows for customization, it is often useful to mark bugs found through threat modeling in a way that makes them easily identifiable. For example, if there is a field that describes how the bug was found, it should be used to identify threat modeling bugs.

Vulnerabilities vs. Threats

A vulnerability is a known security weakness in a system that results in an adversary gaining a company asset that is advantageous to her. As discussed earlier, vulnerabilities are ways of realizing a threat. In a threat tree, a vulnerability represents a valid unmitigated attack path.

Threat modeling separates the concepts of threats and vulnerabilities because a threat model is, in effect, a security specification for a system. Thus, the threat profile is a description of the *problem space,* where the problem space is defined as the set of adversary goals that the system must prevent. Threats are inherently permanent. This list of threats drives feature design and implementation practices. Vulnerabilities, on the other hand, are instances of susceptibility to a threat. As with other software bugs, vulnerabilities are transitory; they can be fixed, freeing the system of the issue.

Identifying Vulnerabilities

Figure 5-7 uses the office building example to illustrate a threat in which an adversary gains entry into the building. An unlocked window is a specific vulnerability; however, this vulnerability can be remedied simply by ensuring that all windows are locked after business hours.

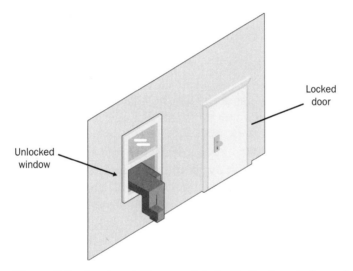

Locked
door

Unlocked
window

Figure 5-7   A vulnerability associated with the threat of an adversary gaining entry to an office building.

The peer-to-peer network application in Figure 5-8 illustrates another example of the relationship between threats and vulnerabilities. A threat to the system exists if the adversary can break the network into many disjoint networks, which would render nodes unable to communicate. A vulnerability exists if disconnect messages sent to peers are not authenticated. Thus, an attacking system could spoof disconnect messages to key peers as though the messages had come from other nodes, which would disrupt the network. As with the office building example, the threat will always exist but the vulnerability can be fixed, in this case, by authenticating messages in a secure manner to ensure they came from the peer node that they claim to come from.

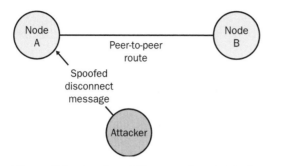

Figure 5-8 A vulnerability associated with the threat of an adversary disrupting a peer-to-peer network.

> **Note** A benefit to noting vulnerabilities in threat model documents along with the system's bug database is that they can be easily collated and used as an instruction tool, both for secure coding and as an aid for constructing new threat models. However, do not let the vulnerabilities listed in the threat model document serve as a substitute for entries in a bug database. An application should have a separate bug database where all of the system's bugs are tracked. Vulnerabilities are simply bugs with security implications. Not tracking them in the usual bug database could result in their not being tracked at all or forgotten about.

Relevance to the Threat Model

- **Who uses the information?** Vulnerabilities are entered as bugs for the system, both in the threat model and in the system's bug database. Designers and implementers must fix or mitigate these bugs. Security testers can use vulnerabilities to look for similar problems in the system or to create regression tests.

- **How is the information collected?** Vulnerabilities are collected by analyzing the enumerated threats and determining which threats have insufficient mitigation. This can be done by using threat trees or other techniques such as code reviews and penetration testing.

■ **How is this information used in the rest of the threat model?** Vulnerabilities are an output of the threat modeling process. While they are not used as in input to the other stages in the threat modeling process, they are used in other areas. For example, vulnerabilities identified in one component might occur in other components also. And, during testing, software testers will write regression tests to ensure that vulnerabilities are fixed and that subsequent revisions of the system do not re-introduce the issue. Finally, reviewers can determine how effective the threat modeling process was by analyzing vulnerabilities found.

Data to Collect

To identify vulnerabilities, the threat modeling team should gather the following information:

■ **Numerical ID**   A unique number should be assigned to the vulnerability.

■ **Name**   This short title for the vulnerability can either be the same as the corresponding threat title or—if multiple vulnerabilities exist for the same threat—can include information about the specific attack path. An example of this would be, "Retrieval of another user's personal data by guessing the user ID on the details Web page."

■ **Description**   The attack path that the vulnerability represents should be described in the description field, providing details about how an adversary would exploit the issue.

■ **DREAD rating**   The vulnerability's risk should be quantified by using the DREAD rating method discussed earlier.

■ **Corresponding threat**   The corresponding threat should be cross-referenced for tracking.

■ **Bug ID**   Because software bugs are tracked in a separate database, the software bug ID for the vulnerability should be listed.

Example: Fabrikam Phone 1.0

Table 5-7 shows an example of a vulnerability for the Fabrikam Phone 1.0 application. The table documents the problem of not changing the default password for the remote administration interface. Note that specific remediation information is best tracked in the bug database associated with the product.

Table 5-7 Fabrikam Phone 1.0 Vulnerability

ID	1
Name	A user gains access to the administration interface.
Description	If the default password is left unchanged and the remote administration interface is enabled, remote anonymous users can easily obtain access to the interface.
STRIDE classification	■ Tampering ■ Information disclosure ■ Denial of service ■ Elevation of privilege
DREAD rating	7.6
Corresponding threat	(1) Adversary gains access to the remote administration interface resulting in access to the phone configuration.
Bug	2122

Example: Humongous Insurance Price Quote Website

The vulnerability example shown in Table 5-8 depicts a SQL injection problem in the Humongous Insurance Price Quote Website. The specific issue is outlined so that it can be avoided in the future and similar issues can be found. This information can be valuable when training new developers or expanding the threat modeling team.

Table 5-8 Humongous Insurance Price Quote Website Vulnerability

ID	1
Name	*RetrieveCredentials* SQL injection
Description	The *RetrieveCredentials* procedure concatenates the *@username* parameter to a SELECT statement: `EXEC('SELECT Password FROM LoginTable WHERE Username = ' + @username)` Because the *@username* parameter is not validated, an attacker could supply a malicious string that—when concatenated with the rest of the statement and then reparsed by the SQL server—could result in arbitrary queries being run. The *@username* parameter should be sanitized for malicious input, or a parameterized version should be used.
DREAD rating	10
Corresponding threat	(1) Adversary uses SQL special characters or keywords in his input to attempt to execute code on the database server.
Bug	45

Example: A. Datum Access Control API

Table 5-9 shows a vulnerability example for the A. Datum Access Control API in which an integer overflow problem results in a security issue. Notice that the corresponding threat is relatively high level but that it discusses the specific input to be manipulated by the attacker.

Table 5-9   A. Datum Access Control API Vulnerability

ID	2
Name	Integer overflow in path length computation for paths greater than 65,535 characters
Description	The path length is calculated using an unsigned short integer (16 bits). This means that a path longer than 64k will cause integer roll-over so that the calculated length will actually be *ActualLength* MOD 65536. Thus, only one character will be allocated for an actual length of 65,537 characters. When the path is copied, arbitrary memory beyond the one character allocation will be overwritten with the input path.
DREAD rating	10
Corresponding threat	(3) Adversary supplies malicious or malformed data as a path to the library, targeting the path parsing code.
Bug	3354

Implications of Resolving Vulnerabilities

Typically, vulnerabilities should be resolved in the same manner in which system bugs are resolved. However, vulnerabilities have additional implications that must be taken into account. When attempting to resolve vulnerabilities, the development team should ask itself questions such as these:

- **What are the security implications for the end user?**   As security vulnerabilities continue to be highlighted in the media and software community, the implications for end users are important to consider. It is best to assume that the vulnerability will be exploited by an adversary if it is found in the product.

- **Has the product shipped or is the vulnerability present in a previous version that has shipped?**   If so, the product team will need to have a process for distributing critical security patches. It is also possible that an external security researcher will discover the vulnerability before the company that developed the product can ship the patch. It is a good idea to have a security response plan in place for such incidents.

- **Are there workarounds that provide an acceptable level of security?**   Some security issues can be managed through workarounds that, although less than ideal, are sufficient to mitigate the vulnerability.

- **What damage to the corporation's reputation could occur?**   The perception of the corporation in the media and the software user community should be taken into account. Failure to do so overlooks a significant portion of the risk associated with a vulnerability.

- **Would a security fix cause the system to break compatibility?**   If so, the security concern might be significant enough to warrant breaking this compatibility.

Vulnerabilities should be addressed regardless of whether a method of exploiting them has been proven. In some cases, vulnerabilities are identified without a specific exploitation technique being known by the development team. If the asset associated with the vulnerability is particularly important, adversaries will be driven to find a way to exploit the issue.

External mitigating factors, such as operating system or other platform features, should take only a limited role in ranking vulnerabilities. For example, a platform that supports buffer overrun detection, such as stack cookies, should not be cause to leave the buffer overrun vulnerability. The vulnerability still exists and because such protection is often generic, researchers will occasionally find holes in the protection that allow it to be bypassed in certain instances.

Threat trees can be used during vulnerability resolution to identify the conditions that can and cannot be mitigated. In some cases, multiple vulnerabilities can be solved by blocking a single condition. In Figure 5-9, mitigating node 1.2 effectively severs two valid attack paths. Fortunately, relationships such as this are often the most apparent solution. That is, it is usually easy to spot mitigation points that will block multiple attack paths because they are often the logical place to mitigate in the first place.

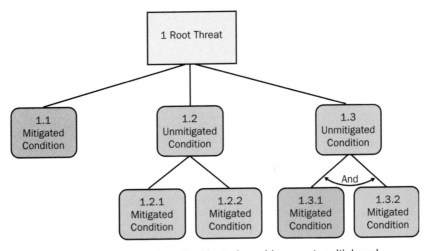

Figure 5-9   One condition that, if mitigated, could prevent multiple vulnerabilities.

Summary

The threat profile defines the security problem space of a system. It outlines the adversary goals that the product development team should prevent by enumerating long-lasting threats to the system's assets. These threats provide the basis and justification for security features and secure coding practices.

Threat modeling teams can understand threats systematically by using threat trees. Utilizing threat trees to analyze threats allows the team to break broad attack goals into individual conditions. This analytical approach enables the team to identify vulnerabilities through attack paths.

Vulnerabilities, or methods of realizing a specific threat, are considered software bugs. Identifying vulnerabilities is an outcome of the threat modeling process, and each threat identified must be analyzed to determine whether it is sufficiently mitigated against.

Part III

Using Threat Modeling Effectively

6

Choosing What to Model

Knowing what features and end-to-end scenarios to threat model and how much detail to include in the documentation is important for effective threat modeling. Ensuring that the most likely attack scenarios are addressed by the threat model is also critical. In addition, because the time and resources needed for thorough security analysis often must be shared with other product development responsibilities, such as designing and implementing the application, development teams must plan threat models in advance and know when the threat modeling process is complete.

Two approaches to threat modeling exist: creating functionality-based, feature-level threat modeling and creating scenario-based, application-level threat modeling. Both approaches are valid, and each has its advantages and disadvantages, as this chapter will show.

This chapter covers the following topics:

- Understanding the difference between feature-level and application-level threat models

- Determining which features and scenarios to threat model

- Knowing when a threat model is complete and what can invalidate a threat model

Creating Feature-Level Threat Models

When threat modeling is tightly integrated into the application-development life cycle, threat models are usually created at the same detail level as specifications. Because specifications typically exist at the feature level, threat models do too. In a feature-level threat model, a feature is the system being modeled. All entry points, even those consumed by other features or components in the application, are considered avenues of attack. Figure 6-1 illustrates how threat models can apply to functional areas of an application. It also depicts how an application-level threat model might consider a remote anonymous user attacking the application via the network. Application-level threat models are discussed later in this chapter.

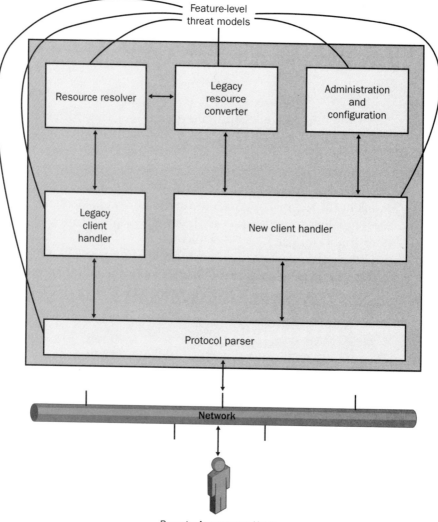

Figure 6-1   Application diagram showing threat models at the feature level and at the application level.

Feature-level threat models are particularly important for high-risk component areas of the application. For example, the access control feature of an application might have more security risk associated with it than a configuration user interface.

> **Tip**   When time and resources are limited, threat modeling only the most critical feature areas rather than all features is a reasonable trade-off.

When it comes to application security, the devil is in the details. Often, vulnerabilities are found in feature areas that do not directly expose functionality to an end user. The product team might have designed and implemented these features while operating under the assumption that no hostile input could be passed to the features because the immediate consumer of their interfaces are other components in the system. However, when threat modeling at the feature level, all entry points to the feature must be cross-referenced with trust levels. Thus, in addition to identifying the consumer of the interfaces, team must identify the original source of the data supplied to the interfaces. For example, a logging feature that can process data from arbitrary sources has a larger threat profile than a feature that only logs static, compiled-in messages.

Benefits of Feature-Level Threat Models

Applying the threat modeling process at the feature level helps ensure robust software. Security analysis that only looks at the application as a whole can fail to scrutinize high-risk features. Such a generalized approach provides breadth but often sacrifices depth. A focused analysis of critical features in separate threat models can ensure that these areas of the application are secure and robust. In addition, feature-specific threats will be much more granular and will not be subject to assumptions about other components in the application.

Feature-level threat models force the whole software development team to think about security; the process must permeate throughout the team. This process pushes the team to develop secure design and implementation procedures. A dedicated team that creates threat models—particularly application-wide threat models—is less likely to cause low-level permeation of the security process because fewer people working on the product will be involved in the security analysis.

Feature-level threat models can provide the background for end-to-end threat models for the system as a whole. In an end-to-end threat model, understanding threats to individual features is a necessary step to understanding how they can be combined with threats to other features. Feature-level threat models also act as feature-specific security specifications that can be referenced during the broader analysis of system threats and vulnerabilities.

Determining Which Features to Model

Most enterprise applications have hundreds, if not thousands, of feature areas. Therefore, threat modeling the right features is critical to using threat modeling resources effectively. Ideally, threat modeling will be well integrated into the development life cycle; threat models are created for every feature at design time and updated through implementation. However, threat modeling every feature is not always possible because of resource constraints. In such cases, only high-risk features should be modeled. Application-level architects are a good resource to assist the threat modeling team in the process.

> **More Info**   The most important aspect in deciding which features to threat model is determining which features will process user-supplied data or otherwise interact with the end user. Chapter 4 discusses using DFDs to describe the threat paths for a system.

Critical feature areas to threat model are those appearing on any of the threat paths for the application as a whole. In addition to using the application-level threat paths to determine features to analyze, some common areas to look at are features that implement:

- **Access control**   Critical in preventing unauthorized disclosure of information, tampering with data and configuration, and numerous other threats.

- **Auditing and logging**   Provide information that can be used to track malicious use.

- **Authentication**   Must provide strong identification mechanisms to thwart impersonation and identity theft.

- **Data format and protocol parsing**   Transform or interpret potentially hostile data from the network, a document file, authentication credentials, e-mail, Web pages, and so on.

- **Permissions**   Grant or deny the user the ability to perform an action.

- **Sandboxes**   Must provide mechanisms to prevent malicious code from escaping a well-defined and confined set of functionality.

- **Session management**   Should be as secure as any initial authentication to prevent hijacking of user sessions in Web applications or other applications.

- **State machines**   Often require certain steps to occur, such as authentication, before transitioning to other states.

Creating Application-Level Threat Models

Application-level threat models, sometimes called *scenario-based threat models,* analyze the application according to a specific deployment and attack scenario. The deployment analysis considers how the application is used by the end user. The attack scenario usually bounds the threat model with specific attack goals, motivations, and characteristics of the adversary. For example, an application-level threat model for a Web server might be constrained by a deployment in which Web Distributed Authoring and Versioning (WebDAV) is enabled but only static Web pages are served and the adversary is a remote anonymous user (a user without credentials on the Web server).

Benefits of Application-Level Threat Models

Application-level threat models are used to discuss end-to-end situations for an application. Entry points, assets, threats, and vulnerabilities should be application-wide, validating security at the application level. These threat models can show how several minor threats against individual features can be aggregated into a much more severe threat at the application level.

The breadth of coverage tends to be wide in the application-level threat model. This is particularly important when feature-level threat models are not created or they are created for only select features.

> **Tip**   The wide breadth of application-level threat models is useful in finding low-hanging fruit—issues that independent security researchers are likely to find first.

Finally, application-level threat models can identify areas in the application that need more in-depth analysis, which often results in finding areas that require feature-level analysis. When threat modeling time and resources are limited, it is a good idea to create application-level threat models for the application first and use these to drive threat models at the feature level for identified high-risk areas. A drawback to this top-down approach is that the features along a threat path must be identified during the application-level threat model.

> **Tip**   In some cases, the bottom-up approach (creating feature-level threat models first and then applying the information to application-level threat models) is preferable. This is because working from the bottom up forces the application-level model to determine how each feature in the application fits into the application threat paths.

Determining Which Applications to Model

Application-level threat models should cover common deployment configurations. This is information that the application team likely will have readily available. Do consider whether to include aspects of the deployment beyond the configuration of the application itself. For example, such consideration must be given to an application that is commonly deployed behind a firewall to prevent access from the general Internet. The application itself cannot control how the firewall is configured or even the fact that the application resides behind a firewall. The threat modeling team might want to ignore this aspect of deployment and focus only on application-controlled configuration, such as whether a particular functionality of the application is enabled.

Application-level threat models should cover adversaries with the least amount of access to the system. This often means addressing the remote anonymous user in threat models (see sidebar). Considering all the functionality that such a user can exercise ensures that a threat model covers the broadest base of potential attackers. As the access categories increase in requisite preconditions (authentication, group membership, proximity, and so on), the number of potential attackers decreases.

The Remote Anonymous User

The remote anonymous user is the most important adversary to consider when doing any security analysis. As the name implies, this user will attack the system remotely, usually via the network, and without supplying credentials. This category of user encompasses the broadest demographic.

Consider the fact that most Internet worms work because of a vulnerability in a remotely accessible interface that does not require authentication. (Note that some worms—mostly those affecting intranets—use authenticated mechanisms to spread, but these are few by comparison.) Such Internet worms have led to an estimated loss of millions of dollars in commerce, productivity, and the like. Because they propagate by using anonymous interfaces, virtually every machine running the affected software or platform on the Internet could be used as an attack base. However, these worms would cause less damage if the vulnerabilities they use to spread the virus reside in an interface that only authenticated users can exploit. This is primarily because fewer potential attackers (those with credentials) exist.

Historical vulnerability information about the application and applications similar to it should be used to drive application-level threat models. Security mailing lists, websites, publications, and other resources detail attacks on a wide range of applications. Threat model teams should consult this information when creating application-level threat models to see how both independent security researchers and malicious users are attacking the application.

Note   Client applications can also have threat models at the system level.

Application-level threat models for client-based applications (such as a word processor) sometimes differ from other application-level threat models because they require a user action, such as opening a document sent via e-mail. Determining which user behavior is "in bounds" for these scenarios is critical. Some user behavior will always result in application insecurity and must be considered out of bounds. However, for any given user action, a threat model team can identify results that should not occur. For example, opening a document—even one sent by a malicious user—in a word processor should not allow an attacker's arbitrary code to run. Such information can be used to drive application-level threat models in client applications.

Choosing the Depth of the Analysis

A common question is how in depth the threat model analysis should be—in other words, how granular a threat model should be. In the perfect world, a threat model would be as granular as necessary to cover individual inputs to each entry point in the system. Threat models falling short of this will miss important threats and often will overlook vulnerabilities.

Keep in mind, however, that some granularity should be reserved for feature-level threat models. For example, if an entry point takes structured data represented as a sequence, the parsing of that structured data might belong in the threat model for the protocol parser feature area. On the other hand, the application-level threat model might be more concerned with how the application uses the data and less concerned with how the parser behaves when it receives malformed data.

A key aspect of determining the depth of analysis is balancing the time and effort spent on the threat model with the level of risk. Focus on high-risk scenarios and high-risk threats first. As the application team becomes more familiar with the threat modeling process, they will become better at circumventing tangential discussions and maintaining the appropriate depth of analysis.

> **Important**   Although a threat model should cover individual inputs to each entry point in the system, in the real world, some granularity must be reserved for feature-level threat models.

Code Review

Determining the depth of analysis for a threat model also involves determining how much work to perform during threat investigations. Some of these investigations are best performed with a code review—for example, the investigation of threats against a protocol parser. Code review is a good investigation technique for threats targeting a constrained part of the application code, as well as threats targeting code that is complex and therefore prone to human error. Furthermore, code review can be helpful when the threat is implementation related and would normally be countered by secure coding practices.

Security Pushes

If the application-level threat model is high level, investigating the threats might be best performed during a security push. In this case, investigation is deferred until time can be dedicated for the entire application team to focus on security. High-level threat models often feed into security pushes, resulting in a depth of analysis dependent on the amount of time dedicated to the push. Although this approach is not a purist one (security analysis is bounded by time rather than depth), security pushes can be extended if the system is found to be insecure.

Penetration Testing

Penetration testing can be used to investigate threats for application-level threat models. Penetration testing is a simulation of an adversary's outside-in analysis and attack on a system. As with a security push, penetration testing often involves time constraints. However, such testing can be useful when code review is too costly in terms of time and resources or not possible because of developer attrition.

> **More Info**   For detailed information about network-based penetration testing, see *Assessing Network Security* by Kevin Lam, David LeBlanc, and Ben Smith from the Microsoft Security Team (Microsoft Press, 2004).

Knowing When a Threat Model Is Finished

To tightly integrate threat modeling into the application-development life cycle, completion criteria for threat models must be established. Tying threat models to software milestones is an effective way of managing their completion, but only if the exit criteria for threat models is clear. The following specific tasks must be finished for a threat model to be complete. Overlooking these tasks is missing the point of threat modeling.

- Document all entry points.

- Resolve all threats.

- Review the threat model documentation.

Threat model completion criteria are key to ensuring that the threat modeling effort results in useful analysis. Such completion criteria also provide clear goals for the threat modeling team so that they can better manage their time. Furthermore, establishing these criteria helps create a standard quality across various threat modeling teams in an organization.

Documenting Entry Points

A finished threat model documents all entry points, the gates that an adversary must use to attack the system. Failing to document an entry point means that it was probably not considered during the threat modeling process. This oversight could ultimately result in missed vulnerabilities. Although documenting all the system's entry points does not imply that the system is secure, it does show that each entry point was considered during the security analysis.

Resolving All Threats

A finished threat model has no unresolved threats. The existence of an unresolved threat means that the security of the system cannot be quantified and implies that mitigation for the threat is unknown. Understanding the system's threat profile is important; understanding how protected the system is against those threats before the product ships is even more important. For the system to be as secure as possible, threats must be both understood and mitigated.

> **Important**   Achieving quantifiable security against a baseline of possible attacks is the driving force behind threat modeling.

Reviewing the Threat Model

A finished threat model document has been peer reviewed, typically by a group of the most security-conscious members of the development team. Depth of analysis is the part of threat model completion that is most subjective. The threat model team must set a minimum bar for how deep the threat model analysis should be and enforce those standards by review. The review process ensures the quality of threat models and provides feedback on the threat modeling process to the modeling team. This feedback is used for further education or to streamline and tailor the threat modeling process to the application team's environment.

Preventing Threat Model Invalidation

Threat modeling teams need to be aware of the factors that can invalidate a threat model. Threat models are considered valid as long as the system remains in a steady state. Various events, both internal and external, affect that state. A threat model is invalidated when the system design or implementation changes. Adding, removing, or modifying functionality can also change the possible threats to a system. Also note that mitigation for threats that remain constant could change. Any modifications to the system must be analyzed by the threat modeling team to determine their impact on the threat model.

> **Note**   A threat model needs updating when a use scenario or external dependency is broken, or changed. Because use scenarios and external dependencies can be used for threat mitigation, a broken use scenario or external dependency implies that the security of the system has changed.

A threat model is also invalidated when a vulnerability is reported externally. If this occurs, the threat modeling team must revisit the threat model to determine which of the following scenarios occurred:

- A threat that encompassed this vulnerability was in the threat model document, but this particular method of realizing the attack goal was not discovered.

- A corresponding threat was never enumerated.

In either of these cases, a post-mortem analysis should be performed to determine how to catch this type of problem in the future and determine any new analysis to perform in similar areas of the application or in other threat models.

Questions Threat Model Teams Should Pose

For completeness, threat modeling teams should consider the questions in this section when creating or reviewing a threat model document.

Overall Description

Threat model documents should include a short description that explains what the component or system is and how it fits into the broader picture. In addition, the overall content of the threat model should provide a clear picture of the system's threat profile. This should be reviewed at the beginning of the threat modeling process and subsequently when the threat model is completed. Threat modeling teams should ask themselves these questions about a model's overall description and content:

- Does the description indicate the purpose of the application or component and how it fits in to the rest of the system?

- Does the description include a link to the current specification?

- Does the language represent the level of effort the threat modeling team put into the analysis of the component's security and how the component's use can affect the overall security of the system?

- Does the description justify all the security features present in the system (such as access control, link/full stack walk demands for .NET assemblies, string/data validation, and so on)?

- Could the document be used to focus a code review for the component?

- Are the threat modeling document and source code consistent and aligned?

- Have all entry points and elements of functionality been considered?

- Does the document contain issues that are not marked as resolved?

- Where was the boundary for the component? Does this boundary include all functionality that is logically part of the component? (For example, a managed class library with some native implementation code should consider that code part of the system being modeled.) In other words, does the system contain functionality that will be missed if this threat model does not cover it?

- Does the document translate easily into a penetration test plan to ensure all threats are mitigated and determine whether any threats were missed? Also, does the document enable a third party to scope an effort to verify the security of the component?

Background Information

The background information in a threat model, discussed in Chapter 4, should be reviewed according to the following criteria:

- Use scenarios
- External dependencies
- Implementation assumptions
- External security notes
- Internal security notes

Use Scenarios

Use scenarios bound the threat modeling discussion and point out scenarios that lie beyond the application's security architecture. These scenarios can also be used as mitigation later in the threat modeling process. Threat modeling teams should ask themselves these questions about use scenarios:

- How is the component or system intended to be used?
- How is it *not* intended to be used?
- How could the use or deployment of the component affect the system's overall security?

External Dependencies

External dependencies must be verified for the threat model to be complete and for potential vulnerabilities to be prevented. Threat modeling teams should ask themselves these questions about external dependencies:

- Which dependencies on external components or systems impact security?
- What assumptions about their behavior are made?
- Does the document identify verifiable information?
- Is it possible to verify that the dependency does not break security via a code review, design review, and so on? Has this been verified and documented by the threat model team?
- Could any changes expected in the other component (or this component) affect this dependency in later milestones?

Implementation Assumptions

Implementation assumptions provide notes to the developer when threat modeling is performed before implementation is complete. The implemented system must be compared with any implementation assumptions to ensure that vulnerabilities were not introduced by not adhering to these notes. Threat modeling teams should ask themselves these questions about implementation assumptions:

- Have any parts of the component not been implemented yet? If so, are security concerns documented regarding these parts?

- When are these features expected to be finished?

- When are these features expected to be included in the threat model?

- For features with implementation assumptions that are now code-complete, have the implementation assumptions been validated in the code?

External Security Notes

External security notes provide valuable security information to end users or consumers of a component. Threat modeling teams should ask themselves these questions about external security notes:

- What usage information should those who consume the component or system consider to prevent security vulnerabilities in their code?

- What inner workings of the component are important for a user to know about?

- How might the component be used incorrectly?

- What positive assumptions can a consumer of the component or system make about the system?

- What functionality or assets can the consumer rely on the component or system to do or protect?

Internal Security Notes

Internal security notes document information relevant to readers of the threat model document, typically in the form of security trade-offs made for business reasons. This next list of questions addresses the internal, post-implementation assumptions threat modeling teams might make regarding internal security notes:

- What information not addressed in the previous lists should some-one reading the threat modeling document know about? (For exam-ple, were security trade-offs made to remain backward compatible?)

- Are there trade-offs between security and performance?

- Do any of the internal security notes really represent actual vulnera-bilities that are not documented as such? If so, the threat model must be revised to document these as vulnerabilities.

The Adversary's View of the System

The adversary's view of the system, discussed in Chapter 3, describes the entry points an adversary can use to attack the system and the assets of interest to her. When reviewing this information in the threat model document, the team should consider entry points, assets, and trust levels.

Entry Points

Entry points show all the places where the adversary can attack the system. Threat modeling teams can prioritize threat discussions by asking themselves what privilege (trust level) an external entity should have to legitimately use an entry point or some functionality at the entry point. These questions can help teams zero in on this information:

- How does data enter the component?

- How can an adversary interface with the component?

- Do the answers to the two previous questions adequately describe the component boundary?

- Is the functionality at each entry point documented?

- Is the user input at each entry point defined?

- Does the description of the entry point identify what processing the system does on behalf of the user at that entry point?

Assets

A threat cannot exist without a corresponding protected resource. Threat mod-eling teams should ask themselves what assets the component or system has that an adversary might try to influence. These can be definite, such as a pro-cess token, or more abstract, such as data integrity. The following questions can help teams identify this information:

■   What data does the system contain that might be of value to an adversary?

■   Does the system have any abilities or rights that the adversary does not?

■   How could an adversary gain from attacking the system?

■   What privilege (trust level) should an external entity have to legitimately influence these assets?

Trust Levels

Trust levels are often broken down by threat modeling teams according to privileges assigned or credentials supplied. They also are cross-referenced with entry points and assets. Teams creating threat models should ask themselves these questions:

■   Are the trust levels documented?

■   Do they say something definitive about either the user interfacing with an entry point or the origin of the data supplied to an entry point?

■   If an entry point is a managed class library such as a .NET assembly, does it document the various security demands that are made and cross-reference those demands with individual APIs?

Modeling the System

Threat model teams should use data flow diagrams (DFDs) or other process models to visually represent how a system processes data. This helps teams predict what an adversary might do at any given entry point. When modeling the system, threat model teams should ask themselves the following questions:

■   Does the context diagram show all the entry points and trust boundaries?

■   Does the context diagram show how the component fits into the rest of the system?

■   What processing occurs beyond an entry point?

■   What task is performed on behalf of the external entity, or what transformation is performed on the data supplied?

■   How are assets affected when performing this task?

■   Where could an external entity manipulate an asset?

Threat Determination

Threats that are not mitigated may become vulnerabilities. Vulnerabilities are a specific manifestation of, or method of realizing, a threat. The questions in this section will help threat modeling teams document a system's potential vulnerabilities.

Identification

To identify threats, determine how an adversary might try to affect an asset for each entry point. The following questions can help:

- What might the adversary try to do to the protected resources or system assets?

- What goals would an adversary have?

- Are these goals realistic?

- Are these goals specific enough that the threat model team could investigate and determine whether a vulnerability exists?

- Have these goals been investigated?

- What was the mitigation of these goals?

- Do they explain what an adversary is trying to do with respect to the enumerated protected resources?

- Have all entry points been considered?

- Are there threats that justify *all* current or planned security features for this application or component?

Vulnerabilities

Vulnerabilities are software bugs that allow the adversary to realize an attack goal. As software bugs, they should be tracked in the application's bug database. However, they should be documented in the threat model document to provide a complete picture of the application's security and how effective the threat modeling process was. The following questions can help threat modeling teams pinpoint system vulnerabilities.

- Do these vulnerabilities correspond to a threat?

- Does a clear correlation exist to explain how each vulnerability is a specific instance of the way the relevant threat could be realized?

- Are these vulnerabilities documented?

- Have they been categorized (via STRIDE classification)?

- Did any issues arise from the threat modeling meetings that have not been documented and were not fixed? The point is not to police the development team. Instead, the point is simply to prevent similar issues from arising in the future by ensuring that threats and vulnerabilities are properly documented in the threat model document. This is not policing; this is simply to prevent similar issues in the future.

Summary

Threat models can be created at both the feature level and the application level. Ideally, a development team creates both types of threat models because each has its advantages and disadvantages. Feature-level threat models are often created at the same granularity as specifications. Application-level threat models take into account common end-user scenarios and specific characteristics and motivations of an external adversary. In either case, prioritizing based on the highest-risk components and scenarios is critical.

A threat model is complete only when it explores all entry points and threats and has been reviewed by all team members. Certain events, such as externally reported vulnerabilities, can invalidate a threat model and require that it be revisited. A threat model document must be kept current for the security of the system to be understood.

7

Testing Based on a Threat Model

Threat modeling is a component in the broader application security life cycle—it does not exist independently of this security life cycle. Guaranteeing the security of a system is impossible. However, testing can provide some assurance of the system's security. When developing a security test plan appropriate for a particular system, the threat modeling team must weigh the plan's required time and effort against the benefits it will yield.

One method of addressing last-minute security testing before a product ships—the security push—involves dedicating time toward the end of the product development life cycle strictly for security testing. Although the security push should not be relied on in lieu of integrated security testing, such a concentrated security effort can be effective at discovering new threats and vulnerabilities. Therefore, the threat modeling team should schedule sufficient time to handle the push output (such as bug fixes) before the product ships.

This chapter covers the following topics:

- Understanding the benefits and shortcomings of security testing

- Using threat models to drive various parts of security testing

- Characterizing the application's security risk

The Benefits and Shortcomings of Security Testing

As Chapter 6 mentioned, testing the security of a system is usually accomplished through design reviews, code reviews, and penetration testing. These testing methods can be used to provide reasonable assurance of the system's security. Conversely, they also can be used to show that the system is of questionable quality. Understanding this practice requires understanding the benefits and shortcomings of this type of testing.

When security testing gets performed is important. Testing prerelease software means that discovered flaws can be fixed before the software ships. On the other hand, testing after shipping can yield difficult business decisions about how to handle identified vulnerabilities and how to present them to users and the media. Finding security vulnerabilities in released software can have significant ramifications for a product's security—and a company's reputation. For one thing, security patches for known vulnerabilities in released products must be provided to the public. In addition, flaws in the system are sometimes discovered and reported externally before the patch has been made available to the public, presenting a public relations dilemma for the software manufacturer. Security testing before a product is released can prevent these vulnerabilities from shipping in the first place.

What Can Security Testing Provide?

Security testing will usually find the low-hanging fruit—the obvious security flaws that an attacker could easily find. This yields two benefits. First, and most obvious, these easily found flaws can be fixed and patched before they are reported externally. The second benefit is more difficult to quantify: When a software vulnerability is publicly reported, security researchers and hackers alike tend to focus on that software. Of course, lots of software without publicly known vulnerabilities tend to be heavily analyzed, too. But existing software vulnerabilities have consistently led third-party researchers and adversaries to focus on the products in question. Finding obvious flaws before they are found externally means that attackers must spend more time and effort attempting to penetrate a system.

Testing is also a quantifiable method to determine whether a security measure or feature works. For instance, a long resource path name supplied in an HTTP request to a Web server could show that overly long path names are handled properly by the system. Combined with code-coverage tools that report code branches reached during testing, security testing would make it possible to see where the malicious request was handled. This could validate, for example, that the request is rejected in the type handler and is not causing corruption in the logging subsystem.

Security flaws found during testing can highlight areas that need more indepth reviews. Data from security reviews shows that where one vulnerability is found, others often exist. Reuse of similar coding constructs, inadequate security design, and inexperience in secure software development can all cause this proliferation of software vulnerabilities. Whatever the reason, the presence of one vulnerability is often an indicator of other software issues—a contributing factor to external researchers focusing on a piece of software with a publicly reported vulnerability.

> **Note**   If penetration testing is used to test the software's security, the tests generated can be reused in the future to ensure that no regressions occur. This requires the penetration testing effort have structure because most informal penetration testing is not focused on creating test cases that could fit into a test harness.

Where Security Testing Fails

Security testing is limited to techniques that are known or discovered by the team during testing. Some testing, such as checking for proper handling of overly long strings, is quantifiable and can be done according to the edge and boundary conditions for the system (for example, testing at the 16-bit integer rollover point, maximum path length, heap allocation granularity, an so on). But not all flaws are as straightforward, either because they are specific to the system being tested and require an element of creativity to discover, or because they are part of a new class of vulnerability. For example, most software products were not reviewed for format string bugs until this type of vulnerability was documented and demonstrated publicly. Although this shortcoming of security testing is not preventable, it shows that keeping up with vulnerability classes is essential to a well-rounded security test.

External attackers and security researchers obviously have different motivations than the development team. Software manufacturers ultimately want to sell secure software—and lots of it. Attackers and researchers, however, are motivated by other desires, often including some that are malicious:

- Damaging the reputation of a company they dislike for whatever reason

- Gaining popularity or fame in the security community or media

- Gaining monetary compensation through direct exploitation of vulnerabilities or blackmail

- Promoting their own "secure" solution

> **Warning**   It is impossible to overestimate an attacker's motivations, which is why the security testing of software companies can never fully predict an adversary's intentions.

Software manufacturers who test software for security are expected to find all vulnerabilities so that they can ship secure products. Attackers need only find one vulnerability to access company assets, which is why they have the advantage over security teams. In reality, security testing teams must choose between *breadth of analysis* and *depth of analysis.* Choosing breadth analysis means that an adversary might only need to make a slightly more concerted effort in one area of the application to find a more complex means of attack than the analysis team predicted. Similarly, if depth is preferred, the adversary might simply look in an area that was not covered by the security review to find a flaw.

> **Note**   Security testing is time consuming, especially when the attacks being simulated are system-specific scenarios. As mentioned, certain tests are relatively easy to quantify. Writing these as repeatable test cases, however, takes time.

How Threat Models Fit In

Threat models are both consumed and revised during security testing. The threat profile described in the threat model document serves as a basis for security testing. Design reviews compare the system's architecture with the threats outlined in the model to ensure that architecture vulnerabilities are mitigated. Code reviews do the same for implementation threats. Penetration tests actively test threats against a running system.

> **More Info**   For more details on threat profiles, see Chapter 5.

Threat models drive security testing by dictating the work plan. They prioritize the areas of analysis and provide high-level tasks in each area. When considering what to test, application-based threat models are a good starting point because the entry points described in such models are accessible to the outside world. Priority should be given to examining the most accessible entry points and testing their functionality.

In addition to general security testing, tasks for a security push include investigating deferred threats from the threat models. When existing applications are threat modeled, some threats might be too broad or too complex to analyze fully during the threat modeling process. The security push can be used to test these threats later so that the threat model can be completed in a timely manner.

The security push is also a good time to review the external dependencies in each threat model. Many times, external dependencies cannot be fully verified until the other components of the application are completed. Because the security push occurs toward the end of the product development cycle, these dependencies can be cross-referenced.

> **Note**   Remember that a system's threat profile, as defined in its threat model document, should describe all the attack goals for a system. A security push—and security testing in general—is governed by these attack goals. The more thorough the threat model, the more straightforward security testing will be.

Using Threat Models to Drive Security Testing

A completed threat model that investigates threats through threat trees is a formal documentation of the ways an adversary might approach attacking a system. Because the point of ensuring product security is to block this malicious use, a finished threat model makes a great basis for a test plan during a security push. A security push—which is performed at the end of the product development life cycle—is typically comprised of testing in three areas:

- Design/threat model reviews
- Code reviews
- Penetration testing

Threat models used in a security push are similar to specifications that must be tested for conformance. The main difference between a threat model used during a security push and a true specification is that in some cases—typically when testing design issues—the test results are subjective. On the other hand, testing for most implementation issues, such as integer overflows and buffer overruns, is a relatively straightforward and objective process.

Design/Threat Model Reviews

Design reviews analyze a system's architecture for security flaws. The focus is on preventing system-specific attacks that target the unique assets of the system. Because a good threat model will cover this information, design reviews during a security push should primarily consist of reviews and updates of existing threat models.

Chapter 6 explained the difference between application-based and feature-based threat models. The security push is a good time to revisit any outstanding systemwide application-based threat models. Ideally such models are completed early in the development cycle. However, revisiting them during the security push ensures that changes made throughout the software development process are taken into account.

Chapter 6 also presents some guidelines for reviewing threat models that can be used during a security push. These should be applied to all a system's application-based and feature-based threat models.

Code Reviews

Security code reviews usually look for vulnerabilities that are countered by secure coding practices. Typically these reviews are not line-by-line audits. Instead, they often follow frequently used code paths, such as logging or parsing routines. The analysis process of a security code review is similar to that of a threat model, following data and process flows from an entry point and analyzing the code for potential issues and flaws.

> **Note** Analyzing all the code branches in security code reviews can be difficult, especially as data is transformed or processed by routines. For this reason, code reviews are often combined with penetration testing. Penetration testing (discussed next) can prove or disprove a theoretical attack quickly, shortening the code review process.

The threat model document, which shows a system's entry points and describes the system's security-critical processing, provides a logical starting point for the code review process. In addition, a threat model aids the code review process by:

- Describing the threats that were considered during application design and implementation

- Allowing the reviewers to revisit the threats to prove or disprove mitigation

- Enabling code reviewers to hypothesize about new threats to the system and determine whether they have been mitigated

Code reviews also serve as a method for investigating threats targeting implementation vulnerabilities. Although the threat modeling team could model an attack and find a buffer overflow by using threat trees, it would be more efficient for them to look for implementation flaws by reviewing code. The threat model is critical in identifying such flaws because it directs the code review to certain sections of code based on an adversary's goals (the assets she wants to target).

Penetration Testing

The definition of penetration testing is straightforward: *the simulation of an adversary's attempts to achieve specific malicious goals in the system.* This simulation includes three phases: the exploratory, flaw identification, and exploitation phases. In software security testing, the exploitation phase is often truncated, for reasons discussed later in this section.

Penetration testing is the most nebulous type of security testing because its process varies widely. It can range from simply running commercial scanning tools, to informal poking around, to a more formal process based on hypothesis or fault testing. Many times when penetration tests are performed, the results are simply a list of vulnerabilities; the specific tests and process used are not disclosed. In contrast, software development teams perform design and code reviews every day, usually to a known process and standard. In a security push, these development teams focus on security. Penetration testing, however, is not as much of an ingrained process. Although similar to software testing, which aims to prove that a product works as it should, penetration testing concentrates on isolating software flaws. In other words, software testing usually verifies that products work in certain scenarios or conditions. This is known as *positive testing.* Penetration testing, on the other hand, detects failures in the code and is therefore considered *negative testing.*

> **Note** Penetration testing can either be *blind* or *informed.* In blind penetration tests, the test team is given no insider knowledge, such as design documentation or source code. With informed penetration testing, the team is given access to some or all of this information.

The Exploratory Phase

In the *exploratory phase* of a penetration test, a system's entry points and their functionality are identified. Informed penetration tests can gather this information from the threat model. Blind penetration tests, however, rely on monitoring tools, probing, reverse engineering, and retail product documentation to find the entry points. To save time, this phase is often informed, even if the flaw identification phase (discussed next) is not.

In penetration testing, the system entry points are the same as those identified during threat modeling. Moreover, preconditions for accessing those entry points (for example, having the ability to write data to the local file system) were identified during the threat modeling process, when the entry points were cross-referenced with trust levels. Penetration test teams use these preconditions to prioritize which entry points to analyze first or in the most detail.

The Flaw Identification Phase

In the *flaw identification phase,* testers perform active testing of a system. Testing for flaws can be either *directed* or *semi-random.* Directed tests attempt to bypass specific security measures to achieve a goal. However, semi-random tests—typically performed by fuzzing (manipulating a format or protocol to test boundary conditions or elicit errors in the application)—are often done when a file format or protocol is being tested.

For example, a directed test for a Web application might involve acquiring a valid session identifier and then modifying the account number in a URL. This would determine whether sufficient access checking in the system exists to prevent one user from accessing another user's account information. The result of this test might show that access control is not performed beyond checking whether the user has a valid session identifier.

On the other hand, semi-random testing through fuzzing explores the edge conditions of a format or protocol. That is, fuzzing should test limits such as buffer sizes, integer rollover points, handling of negative numbers, incorrect state transitions, or otherwise inject unexpected data into the system. For example, such testing might expand buffer and string lengths, change the values of embedded integer values, send incomplete data, or perform partial handshaking in a somewhat random fashion to find flaws. This sort of testing typically has a random element to it, trying different conditions together or in sequence to evoke system errors. Semi-random testing requires less maintenance on the part of the tester; the tester simply creates a fuzzer for the system and runs it, waiting for the system to fail.

The Exploitation Phase

In the *exploitation phase,* working exploits of discovered flaws are developed to demonstrate how an adversary could achieve one of his goals. This phase is common when a product development team works with a third-party security consultancy. In such relationships, proof of exploitability is often a requirement for the consultancy to justify the recommended security fix. Internal penetration testing teams often skip this phase in favor of directly addressing the flaw.

Another reason for skipping this phase is that the product development team already knows about these exploits. For example, buffer overflows on both the stack and the heap are known to be exploitable in most situations. Rather than coding an exploit for a specific flaw, it is more efficient to simply fix it.

> **Caution**   As the difficulty of fixing the flaw increases, either because of costs or compatibility issues, proof of exploitability is sometimes required to justify the fix to management.

Characterizing the Application's Security Risk

The likelihood of a severe, exploitable security vulnerability being discovered amounts to a system's security risk. Threat modeling and security testing can be used to gauge the relative risk of the application by showing its strengths and weaknesses. An application's security strengths are proven measures that counter threats. Application weaknesses are deficiencies that lead to partially or wholly unmitigated threats. Summarizing the strengths and weaknesses in a meaningful way requires metrics that are often subjective. However, using classifications such as STRIDE and DREAD, both of which were introduced in Chapter 5, can help.

Application Strengths

Showing that software is resilient to attacks is often pushed aside to simply enumerate vulnerabilities in the system. This can result in an inaccurate perception of risk in software that is otherwise secure. Such misrepresentation of an application's security risk is akin to listing only the class subjects in which a student is failing on a report card. If the student is struggling in a single class but excelling in the others, such a report card does not give an accurate portrayal of the student's abilities.

The threat modeling process described in this book ensures that system strengths are noted in the threat modeling documentation. Each feature, technique, or mitigation for a threat is a strength. In security testing, strengths are noted by a tester's inability to break the security of the software. Describing the strengths of an application shows what components were tested. This information is especially valuable for a system in which few or no vulnerabilities are discovered. Having such information prevents retesting and further demonstrates the software's ability to withstand attacks. In cases where the justifiability of software security testing is in question, describing the application strengths evidenced through testing can be valuable.

Application Weaknesses

The weaknesses of a system are not just an enumeration of vulnerabilities discovered. To be meaningful, system weaknesses, or vulnerabilities, must also take into account their effects on security (by using the STRIDE model) and the risk associated with their exploitation (by using the DREAD model).

As with vulnerabilities discovered during the threat modeling process, vulnerabilities discovered during security testing can utilize the STRIDE and DREAD classifications. Because vulnerabilities found through security testing will already have a threat associated with them in the threat model or the threat model will need to be revised to include a new threat, vulnerabilities can be retrofit into the model to provide a single data source for characterizing weaknesses.

A useful way of providing a numerical assessment of weaknesses is to first categorize vulnerabilities according to the threat's primary STRIDE category and then give a composite DREAD rating. For example, a system might have 20 elevation of privilege threats identified, 2 of which have vulnerabilities associated with them. Assuming a DREAD range of 0 to 3, the average rating would be 1. Figure 7-1 illustrates the various threats to a system, in terms of their DREAD rating.

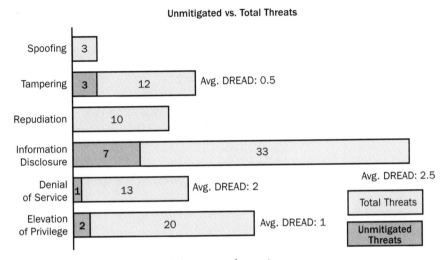

Figure 7-1   The composite weaknesses of a system.

In threat modeling, more than one vulnerability can be associated with a single threat. This is why the composite rating for each threat in the figure compares unmitigated threats to total threats, rather than vulnerabilities to threats. The latter comparison does not provide a useful number because the vulnerability count could exceed the threat count. However, the vulnerability count is still important.

For example, if one of the unmitigated threats to the system in Figure 7-1 has 10 unique attack paths (and therefore 10 vulnerabilities), the system probably has some serious issues that the composite rating does not indicate. Adding an average vulnerability rate to the unmitigated ratio will help show this, especially when few unmitigated threats but a large number of vulnerabilities exist. Although this number is diluted as more threats are unmitigated, it is balanced by the fact that the unmitigated ratio goes up. Figure 7-2 shows a system's composite weakness rating in terms of its threats' DREAD ratings.

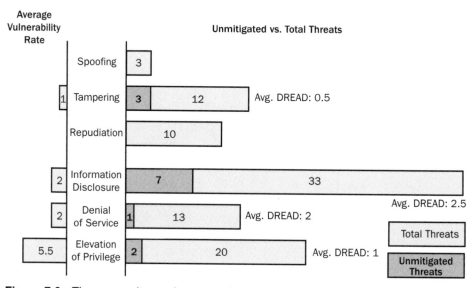

Figure 7-2   The composite weaknesses of a system, with the average vulnerability rating included.

Determining the Effectiveness of Threat Modeling and Security Testing

Application security is often judged based on the number of vulnerabilities found. Certainly, finding a large number of vulnerabilities or several high-impact vulnerabilities can be used to justify time and resources spent on application security. However, uncovering a lack of vulnerabilities during the application security process does not mean that threat modeling or security testing failed. Rather, this is evidence that the overall security process is succeeding. Through threat modeling and security testing, the development team can show that their software is robust and low in security risks.

Characterizing the strengths and weaknesses of the system as described in this chapter provides a great deal of feedback on the application security life cycle to the development team. However, the effectiveness of the security process can be difficult to measure until the software has been on the market for months or even years. Vulnerabilities being publicly reported only a short time after the product is released can mean deficiencies in the security process exist. On the other hand, an increase in the time to first vulnerability (the period from when the software is released to the first public announcement of a vulnerability) often serves as an indication of a good security process.

Time to first vulnerability is best compared to historical data for the product. This information gives a relative comparison of product security and allows product managers to view the process as improving or deteriorating. Of course, time to first vulnerability is only one aspect of measuring software security. The severity of the vulnerability, average time to vulnerability (mean of the periods from release to each publicly announced vulnerability), and total vulnerability count should also be analyzed.

Summary

Threat models can be used to drive security testing. Because a threat model describes all an adversary's attack goals through the threat profile, the testing can be confined, allowing an organized work plan. Security testing can be used to investigate outstanding threats or to test mitigation of product vulnerabilities.

Security testing also can show that a product is resilient with regard to attacks or that it has serious defects. In either case, the value of security testing should not be overlooked. The number of vulnerabilities discovered in a product is not the only result that makes security testing valuable. In addition, increased confidence in the quality of the product helps prove that the overall security process is working, adding value to the security testing performed.

Making Threat Modeling Work

To make the most of the time a product development team invests in threat modeling, the whole team needs to be involved. In addition, the individuals involved need to understand the approach and the goals of creating the threat model. An understanding of secure programming fundamentals helps tremendously, although it is not necessary; a development team familiar with the methodology described in this book can easily create a successful threat model.

This chapter covers the following topics:

- Considering the practicalities of threat modeling
- Revisiting a threat model throughout product development—and in the future
- Getting additional help with securing software products
- Managing the threat modeling process

Practical Considerations

Assessing and documenting security vulnerabilities lie at the core of threat modeling. This information is then used to mitigate those vulnerabilities and improve the security of the feature or application. The earlier vulnerabilities are found, the more cost effective it is to fix them.

Consider the average patch for a deployed software product—it costs a lot of money to ship a patch. It costs even more for customers to test and install a patch in their computing environments. Architectural issues are the most expensive and difficult for the development team to fix. Every security issue found during the development process is one more patch that does not have to be shipped. Threat modeling an application identifies its architectural issues and the high-risk areas that will benefit most from implementation-level analysis such as penetration testing and source code review.

To ensure that the application and its customers benefit from the threat modeling process, include threat modeling in the planning, documenting, and scheduling of the development process. Cost is also a critical factor in any project, and the benefit of reducing costs over the application life cycle should be considered.

Planning

Dedicate time to the threat modeling process in the project's development plan. Use the threat models to design security test plans as described in Chapter 7. As development proceeds, ensure that the threat models are updated and the mitigations are still valid. As new threats are introduced, include them in the analysis of the threat model. If new vulnerabilities are found in products similar to the application being analyzed, use the threat model to understand whether those risks are relevant to the application being developed and revise the threat model as needed to keep it current.

Documenting

Use the threat model to document the product. The threat model begins by explaining the risks inherited by the environment. These risks might change from deployment to deployment. Documentation writers will use the threat model to help system administrators understand how to deploy the application in environments with various requirements. The default deployment should be secure, but if the application is deployed in a non-default environment, the risks will change.

Caution   For some deployments, such as those in a small business or home office, traffic in the clear on an internal network might be acceptable. However, this scenario might be unacceptable for a user deploying this application that communicates over the network in an environment with high security requirements, such as the military or a financial institution. If the default configuration is not to use encrypted or otherwise protected network traffic, then the threat model documentation can help identify the default deployment as a risk and suggest alternatives for environments with higher security requirements.

The threat model should be shared with other teams within the company that build or integrate with the application. This allows the other team to verify dependencies and ensure that any assumptions are not incorrect. Many security vulnerabilities occur at integration points between components or applications. Sharing the threat model can catch potential issues arising from assumptions that are not validated.

Scheduling

Threat modeling can be adapted to fit any schedule. The methodology presented in this book is an ideal approach. However, not every project can afford the amount of time needed to perform threat modeling to completion. Therefore, the approach presented in this book is designed to yield results on the highest risk components first and enable in-depth analysis through iterations. Performing threat modeling at even the highest level identifies the areas most at risk and the threat scenarios that must be mitigated first. In-depth analysis is required to fully understand the security architecture of the application, but much value can be gained even if a short amount of time is available for the threat modeling process.

Determining Costs

Even an incomplete threat model is valuable to understanding where an application faces risk. Dedicating only a short amount of time to threat modeling is better than sending the application into the world without any analysis at all.

Architecture security issues are easiest to address when found in the design phase. If discovered early enough, the fix might involve nothing more than reworking a drawing on a whiteboard. However, once the application is implemented, the same problem might take many months to reengineer. If the problem is found during deployment, the fix must be implemented and a patch must be deployed. Figure 8-1 shows how the cost of discovering a security issue increases significantly as the project proceeds.

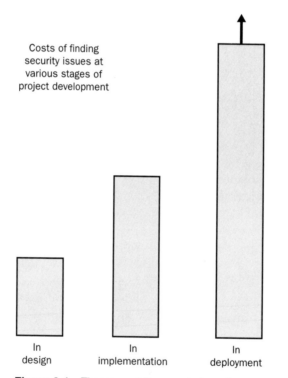

Costs of finding security issues at various stages of project development

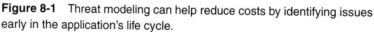

In design   In implementation   In deployment

Figure 8-1   Threat modeling can help reduce costs by identifying issues early in the application's life cycle.

As shown in the figure, the cost of fixing security issues in design is minimal. Costs increase when a security fix is found during the implementation stage; this cost is generally measured in person-months. When a fix is required after the application is deployed, the cost of fixing the issue can be significant and might include:

- Person-months to build and deploy the patch for each affected system

- Monetary costs associated with shipping the patch

- Monetary costs incurred any time the application is unavailable to customers

- Intangible cost of customer dissatisfaction and the possible damage to reputation

The best way to avoid these costs is to implement security in all areas of application development.

> **More Info**   For more information about the return on security investment, read "Tangible ROI Through Secure Software Engineering" by Kevin Soo Hoo, Andrew W. Sudbury, and Andrew R. Jaquith. This article is available online from *Secure Business Quarterly* at *http://www .sbq.com/sbq/rosi/sbq_rosi_software_engineering.pdf*.

Revisiting the Threat Model

The threat model can be used to create security test plans, as discussed in Chapter 7. For the threat model to be effective, it must reflect the actual project implementation. Therefore, maintaining the threat model as the project progresses is key. Anyone who has actually built a large software project understands that implementation is often quite different from design. Some design issues are unclear until implementation. If the threat model is created during the design stage, it needs to be updated as implementation milestones are met. In other words, threat modeling is an iterative process, as illustrated in Figure 8-2.

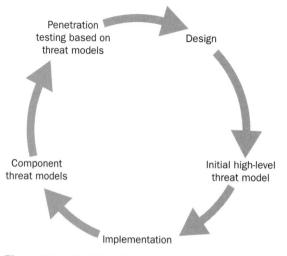

Figure 8-2 Revisiting the threat model.

The threat model should also be used as new versions of the product are considered and the design phase begins again. The threat model identifies the weakest aspects of the security architecture. These are most likely the security aspects that should be addressed when an opportunity to redesign or re-implement arises—for example, when developing a new version of the product. Continually improving security in the application creates a stronger product that can better withstand malicious attacks and builds customer confidence in the security—and therefore the reliability—of the product.

> **Important** Just as implementing a single security feature once will not make an application secure, performing threat modeling once without revisiting the threat model documentation will not secure the application. Applications become more secure when the development team incorporates security into the development process and when everyone on the development team makes it their job to focus on a product's security issues.

Where to Go for Help

Even though the field of application security is fairly new, other resources can help integrate security into a development environment. If the process of threat modeling is still too daunting after reading this book, consider hiring some outside help. Security consulting vendors can help a development team review a design for security issues, with or without employing threat modeling. The most commonly offered services of such consultancies include source code review and penetration testing of the application.

Be sure to ask vendors to describe the methodology they will use to analyze the application. Otherwise, it is can be difficult to determine whether each component has had a thorough examination or whether the vendor spent all the analysis time in places most likely to produce vulnerabilities. In addition, without an awareness of the procedural methodology used, it can be difficult for a development team to pick up where the vendor left off when constructing test cases and getting complete (or as complete as possible) coverage in security testing the application.

Development teams seeking outside help should also avoid vendors that have a haphazard approach to application security. The try-a-bunch-of-things approach might find security issues, but it will not leave the development team members confident that they understand the overall risk for the application.

> **More Info**   *Writing Secure Code, Second Edition* (Microsoft Press, 2003), by Michael Howard and David LeBlanc identifies implementation mistakes that are commonly made. This book is an essential read for developers who want to get up to speed on secure programming practices.

Managing the Threat Modeling Process

Threat modeling should be performed at a high level in the design phase of the product development life cycle and then in more depth after the project is feature complete—in some environments, this can mean after an initial beta is shipped. For large development initiatives, it makes sense to perform threat modeling at the highest level during design and then have each component team perform threat modeling on their respective components as appropriate.

Determining Time Frame

How much time should be spent on threat modeling? The appropriate amount of time depends on the answers to several questions:

■ How complex is the application?

■ How much risk does the application face?

■ Does the application listen on the network?

■ Does the application accept input from high-risk sources? For example, an unauthenticated Web application might be a high-risk resource, while a management interface for administrators might be a low-risk one.

■ Does the application protect valuable resources? For example, a financial transaction system might be considered a more valuable resource than a text editor.

■ Is the security of the application under particular scrutiny? Have vulnerabilities already been found in the application by parties outside the development team?

When deciding how much time to spend threat modeling, plan to spend more time modeling the riskier, more complex applications and less time modeling the applications with fewer moving parts and less risk.

Identifying Vulnerabilities

Just because a product does not yet have any vulnerabilities identified since it was released does not mean vulnerabilities do not exist. It is true that many vulnerabilities are identified by internal development teams, hackers, and third-party researchers that look for them. But it is also true that other vulnerabilities are not found because no one is looking for them.

Many vulnerabilities that are discovered and disclosed publicly have been in code for a very long time. The OpenSSL timing-based SSL/TLS attack that was reported to the Bugtraq security mailing list on February 24, 2003, had been present in a widely deployed code base that was under continuous scrutiny for years. Similarly, the vulnerability in the Microsoft ASN.1 Library that allowed arbitrary code execution (bulletin MS04-007) was found in code that was present as early as Microsoft Windows NT 4.0 Service Pack 6a. Even if developers and security researchers are looking for security bugs, they may be looking for different types of known problems. And if a new class of vulnerability or method of exploit is discovered, past security review will not have investigated for the new bug.

> **More Info**   The Bugtraq security mailing list can be found on the Security Focus website at *http://www.securityfocus.com*.

The development team needs to be aware of the changing security landscape. As new classes of security vulnerabilities are discovered, the team needs to integrate this knowledge into their security analysis. Furthermore, they need to understand how the new vulnerability types affect older software, especially if it is still being used.

Summary

The security of an application cannot be understood, analyzed, or characterized unless the threats to the system are quantified in a threat model document. The methodology presented in this book is designed to help development teams create more secure software for both internal and customer use. Threat modeling can be applied beyond the development environment and can be used to understand the risks of a system deployment or even the physical security risks of an office building, as seen by some of the examples in Chapters 3 through 5.

Business infrastructure relies on software. The reliability of the software impacts business continuity. Security is becoming the most important aspect of reliability because the world is changing. Critical business functions are now being performed over public networks. The public networks are becoming more and more hostile as new techniques to subvert application security are discovered.

Any level of security analysis is better than none. Taking the time to understand the risks an application must be resilient to allows a business to make intelligent choices about securing the assets the application must use and protect.

Part IV

Sample Threat Models

Appendix A

Fabrikam Phone 1.0

The Fabrikam Phone 1.0 sample threat model is intended to present threat modeling concepts without being tied to any particular software or type of application. Fabrikam, Inc. created Phone 1.0 as its first telephone suitable for business applications. This phone has features common to consumer telephones, such as caller ID, speed dial, and an answering machine. In addition, Phone 1.0 includes an access control feature that regulates which users can make calls from the phone and access its administrative features.

Table A-1 contains the high-level information about the threat model being developed for the Fabrikam Phone 1.0. This basic information includes the type of product and its location, the owner of the threat model and its team members, and any available milestone information.

Table A-1   Threat Model Information

Product	Fabrikam Phone 1.0
Milestone	RTM
Owner	Kim Abercrombie
Participants	Alice Ciccu, Scott Gode
Reviewer	John Arthur
Location	Database\Fabrikam Phone 1.0 (Phone 1.0)
Description	The Fabrikam Phone 1.0 (Phone 1.0) is Fabrikam, Inc.'s first high-tech telephone device. The phone includes popular features such as caller ID, speed dial, and an answering machine. In addition, it has features that enable its use in semi-private areas, such as conference rooms.

Use Scenarios

Table A-2 lists the known use scenarios for the application—in other words, the expected use of Phone 1.0. Using or deploying the application in a way that violates its use scenarios could impact its security.

Table A-2 **Use Scenarios**

ID	Description
1	The Fabrikam Phone 1.0 application will be connected to the Public Switched Telephone Network (PSTN). The security of this network is beyond the control of Phone 1.0.
2	If Phone 1.0 is installed in a location that untrusted users can access, the application should have local access control enabled.
3	Fabrikam did not design Phone 1.0 to withstand attacks against the physical device.

External Dependencies

Table A-3 lists the external dependencies Phone 1.0 has on other components or products, which can impact security. Such external dependencies are assumptions made about the usage or behavior of these other components or products. Inconsistencies in these assumptions can lead to security weaknesses.

Table A-3 **External Dependencies**

ID	Description
1	Fabrikam Phone 1.0 depends on the PSTN for providing power. A two-day power cell in Phone 1.0 provides backup power should the power provided by the PSTN go down.

Implementation Assumptions

Table A-4 lists the implementation assumptions of Phone 1.0 and describes each assumption about the internal workings of the application that is made during the specification phase, but before implementation has started. These assumptions should not be violated. Typically, they will be reviewed by the threat model team further once implementation takes place.

Table A-4 **Implementation Assumptions**

ID	Description
1	The voice-command dialing option has yet to be implemented. If added, this option should not introduce a way for adversaries to bypass current security features, such as long-distance call lockout.
2	If encrypted communication is added to the application, key exchange should be done according to industry-accepted standards.

External Security Notes

Table A-5 lists the external security notes, which are threats or other information that an application user should be aware of to prevent possible vulnerabilities. These notes might include features that, if used incorrectly, could cause security problems for application users.

Table A-5 External Security Notes

ID	Description
1	Phone 1.0 has a remote administration interface with a default numeric password. Although the interface is disabled by default, the user should ensure that the password is changed if it the feature is enabled.
2	If the user wants to protect the speed-dial list and protect whether remote administration is enabled, he should enable local access control.
3	The long-distance password can be enabled only when local access control is enabled. Furthermore, entering the long-distance password with the keypad allows local calls to be made.
4	If the user wants to control who can make outgoing calls, local access control should be enabled.

Internal Security Notes

Table A-6 list the internal security notes, which contain security information relevant only to someone reading the threat model. These notes can be used to explain implementation choices and design decisions made due to nonsecurity factors (for example, backward compatibility or overriding business needs) that affect the system's security.

Table A-6 Internal Security Notes

ID	Description
1	Speed-dial information, voice mail messages, and the outgoing greetings are all stored in volatile RAM. Manufacturing the combination of volatile RAM and a battery backup for Phone 1.0 is cheaper than using nonvolatile RAM. However, power loss to Phone 1.0 can cause the loss of information if the battery backup is depleted.

Trust Levels

Table A-7 lists the trust levels and describes privilege levels that are associated with entry points and protected resources.

Table A-7 Trust Levels

ID	Name	Description
1	Administrator	The Phone 1.0 administrator has access to all features and can bypass all security checks.
2	Long-distance user	Phone 1.0 can be configured to restrict long-distance calling. The long-distance user is a phone user permitted to make long-distance calls.
3	Local call user	The local call user can place only outgoing local calls.
4	Denied user	Phone 1.0 can be configured to prevent access to the phone without a password. The denied user is a user with no access.
5	Anonymous remote user	The anonymous remote user represents any data or incoming calls over the PSTN.

Entry Points

Table A-8 list the entry points and describes the interfaces through which external entities can interact with the application, either directly or by indirectly supplying it with data.

Table A-8 Entry Points

ID	Name	Description	Trust Level
1	Handset	Used by the user for voice communication. Voice-activated dialing will also be implemented via this interface.	(1) Administrator (2) Long-distance user (3) Local call user (4) Denied user
2	Keypad	Used for dialing, entering local access passwords, and other administrative functions on Phone 1.0.	(1) Administrator (2) Long-distance user (3) Local call user (4) Denied user
3	Telephone line	Phone 1.0 interfaces with the PSTN via the telephone line.	(5) Anonymous remote user

Table A-8   Entry Points

ID	Name	Description	Trust Level
4	Alpha-numeric display	Shows information such as speed-dial numbers, caller ID, and administrative menus.	(1) Administrator (2) Long-distance user (3) Local call user (4) Denied user
5	Audible ringer	This is an exit point that alerts the user of incoming calls.	(1) Administrator (2) Long-distance user (3) Local call user (4) Denied user
6	Remote administration	This menu-driven interface is accessed remotely over the PSTN. The interface is enabled when the answering-machine feature of Phone 1.0 is enabled and is accessed by pressing the 9 key when the phone answers.	(1) Administrator

Assets

Table A-9 lists the assets and describes the data or functionality that Phone 1.0 needs to protect. The table also lists the minimum trust level that should be allowed to access the resource.

Table A-9   Assets

ID	Name	Description	Trust Level
1	Speed-dial list	Contains the names and numbers of frequently used contacts.	(1) Administrator (2) Long-distance user (3) Local call user
2	Caller ID	Provides information about the incoming caller.	(1) Administrator (2) Long-distance user (3) Local call user
3	Access to the PSTN	Phone 1.0 indirectly protects access to the PSTN.	(1) Administrator (2) Long-distance user (3) Local call user

Table A-9 **Assets**

ID	Name	Description	Trust Level
4	Long-distance calling	Phone 1.0 has optional lockout for long-distance calling so that only authorized users can make long-distance calls.	(1) Administrator (2) Long-distance user
5	Phone configuration	This is the administrative configuration for Phone 1.0.	(1) Administrator
6	Messages	These are messages left by callers when Phone 1.0 has the answering-machine feature enabled.	(1) Administrator (2) Long-distance user (3) Local call user
7	Telephone conversation	The conversation held via Phone 1.0 can contain private information and should be protected.	(1) Administrator (2) Long-distance user (3) Local call user
8	Alertion mechanisms	Includes the audible ringer and flashing LED used to alert the user to incoming calls.	(1) Administrator (2) Long-distance user (3) Local call user
9	Message store	Phone 1.0 stores incoming messages in compressed form on 8 MB of dedicated RAM. The administrator can listen to and delete these messages. The anonymous remote user can leave messages when answering-machine mode is enabled. The message store also houses the outgoing greeting on the phone system.	(1) Administrator (5) Anonymous remote user
10	Outgoing greeting	Phone 1.0 plays this greeting when it answers the phone in answering-machine mode. The administrator has access to change the outgoing greeting. The anonymous remote user hears the greeting when answering-machine mode is enabled.	(1) Administrator (5) Anonymous remote user

Data Flow Diagrams

The Fabrikam Phone 1.0 has two data flow diagrams (DFDs). Figure A-1 shows the context diagram, and Figure A-2 shows the Level 0 diagram. The context diagram depicts the external entities that access Phone 1.0 and its entry points.

The Level 0 diagram shows the data flow for a remote user accessing the administration mode.

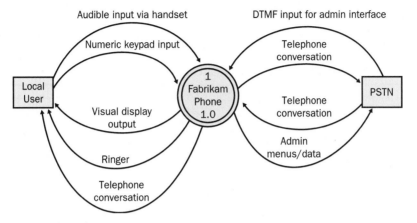

Figure A-1   Context diagram.

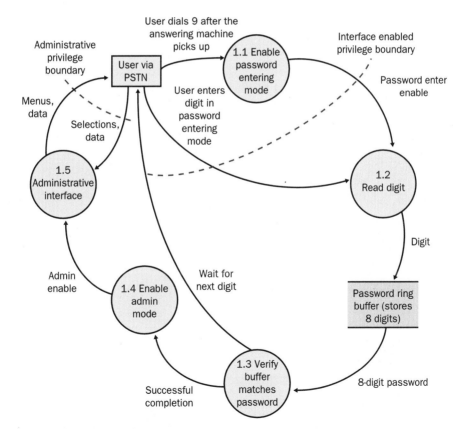

Figure A-2   Level 0 diagram.

Threats

The threats to the application are listed here in a series of tables—one table for each threat. These threats do not imply vulnerabilities. Rather, they are goals that a malicious external entity might have when attacking the system.

Table A-10   Threat: Unauthorized Remote Access

ID	1
Name	Adversary gains access to the remote administration interface, resulting in access to the phone configuration
Description	Phone 1.0 has a remote administration interface that allows an authorized user to configure it via the PSTN. The interface is disabled by default but can be enabled by using the local keypad.
STRIDE classification	■ Tampering ■ Information disclosure ■ Denial of service ■ Elevation of privilege
Mitigated?	No
Known mitigation	If the remote administration interface is enabled, the user should change the default password. *Related external security notes:* (1) Phone 1.0 has a remote administration interface that has a....
Investigation notes	None
Entry points	(6) Remote administration (3) Telephone line (2) Keypad
Assets	(5) Phone configuration

Table A-10   Threat: Unauthorized Remote Access

Threat tree

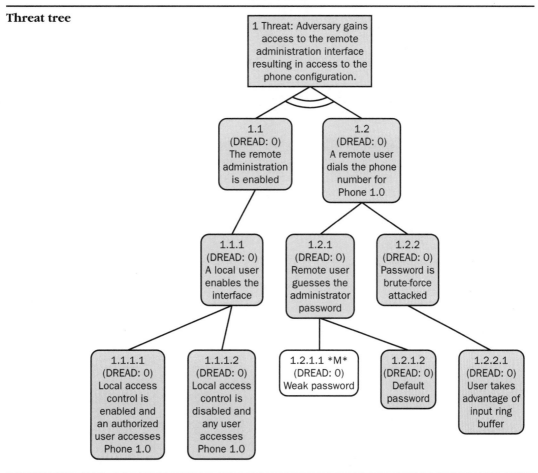

Table A-11   Threat: Speed-Dial List Disclosure

ID	2
Name	Adversary reads the speed-dial list
Description	The speed-dial list has sensitive information (including names and telephone numbers).
STRIDE classification	Information disclosure
Mitigated?	Yes
Known mitigation	If access control is disabled, the speed-dial list cannot be protected. If enabled, brute-force attacks on the password become difficult because the phone requires eight-digit passwords and the passwords are entered via the keypad. Phone 1.0 is not responsible if the password is disclosed by the phone's owner.
	The threat of an adversary trying to read the speed-dial list via the remote administration interface is covered by the threat of an adversary gaining access to that interface.
	Related use scenarios:
	(2) If Phone 1.0 is installed in a location where untrusted users can access it....
	Related external security notes:
	(2) If the user wants to protect the speed-dial list and whether....
Investigation notes	None
Entry points	(2) Keypad
	(4) Alphanumeric display
	(1) Handset
Assets	(1) Speed-dial list

Table A-11   Threat: Speed-Dial List Disclosure

Threat tree

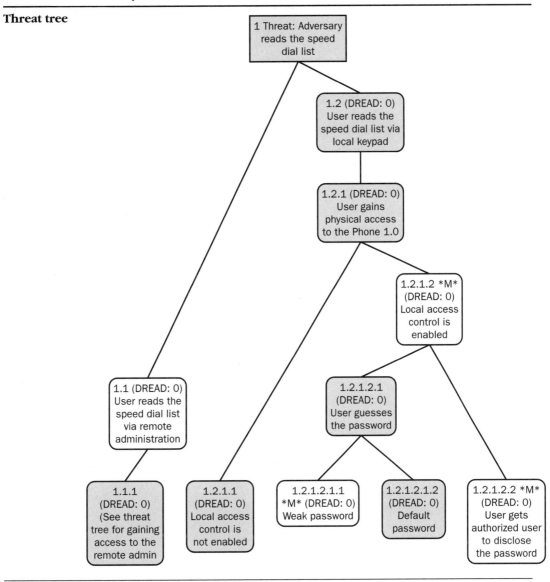

Table A-12   Threat: Unauthorized Long-Distance Call

ID	3
Name	Adversary makes a long-distance call
Description	Access to long distance can be restricted. Often it is not desirable for a company to allow arbitrary users to make long-distance calls.
STRIDE classification	Elevation of privilege
Mitigated?	Yes
Known mitigation	If the local access control is disabled, the long-distance calling capability cannot be protected. If enabled, brute-force attacks on the password become difficult because the phone requires eight-digit passwords and the passwords are entered via the keypad. Phone 1.0 is not responsible if the password is disclosed by the phone's owner.
	If a long-distance password has not been configured and local access control is enabled, the phone defaults to the local access control password for long distance. Local access control must enabled for a long-distance password to be configured. The long-distance password grants all rights that the local call password does.
	Related use scenarios:
	(2) If Phone 1.0 is installed in a location where untrusted users can access it....
	Related external security notes:
	(3) The long-distance password can be enabled only when local access....
Investigation notes	None
Entry points	(1) Handset
	(2) Keypad
Assets	(4) Long-distance calling

Table A-12   Threat: Unauthorized Long-Distance Call

Threat tree

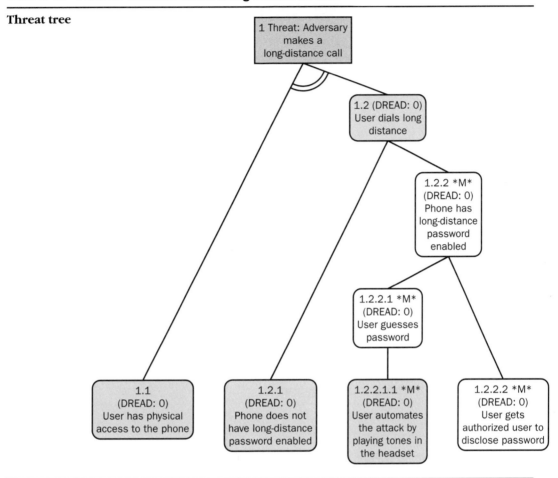

Table A-13   Threat: Disclosure of Caller ID Information

ID	4
Name	Adversary views caller ID information
Description	In some cases, the organization will want to protect caller ID information.
STRIDE classification	Information disclosure
Mitigated?	Yes
Known mitigation	After review, the caller ID information was deemed not sensitive by the threat modeling team. Thus, any user who can view the alphanumeric display can view caller ID data. Given Phone 1.0's current design, the method of protecting caller ID would be to restrict it by using local access control. However, if this method is implemented, the user would have to enter his access code to view the caller ID data for each incoming call.
Investigation notes	To protect caller ID data, Fabrikam would have to use the local access control mode. If this strategy is implemented, the user would have to enter his access code to view the caller ID data for each incoming call. Users likely will not find this requirement user friendly.
Entry points	(4) Alphanumeric display
Assets	(2) Caller ID
Threat tree	None

Table A-14   Threat: Unauthorized Calling

ID	5
Name	Adversary makes an outgoing call
Description	When local access control is enabled, outgoing calls should be restricted to authorized users.
STRIDE classification	Elevation of privilege
Mitigated?	Yes
Known mitigation	Outgoing calls can be restricted only when local access control is enabled. If disabled, the phone has no way to restrict access.
	Related use scenarios:
	(2) If Phone 1.0 is installed in a location where untrusted users can access it….
	Related external security notes:
	(4) If the user wants to control who can make outgoing calls, locate….
Investigation notes	None

Table A-14   Threat: Unauthorized Calling

Entry points	(1) Handset
	(2) Keypad
Assets	(3) Access to the PSTN
Threat tree	

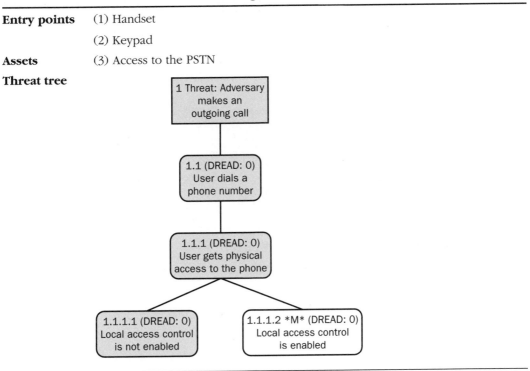

Table A-15   Threat: Modification of the Speed-Dial List

ID	6
Name	Adversary modifies the speed-dial list
Description	If the speed-dial list is modified, an outgoing call could be placed to the wrong number.
STRIDE classification	Tampering
	Elevation of privilege
Mitigated?	Yes

Table A-15 Threat: Modification of the Speed-Dial List

Known mitigation	The remote administration interface is vulnerable and can unwittingly grant adversaries access to the speed-dial list. See Table A-10, which outlines the threat of an adversary gaining access to the remote administration interface, for the relevant vulnerabilities. Because the security of the speed-dial list depends on the security of this interface, the vulnerabilities of the administration interface are not replicated here.
	For local access, a brute-force attack against the administrator password requires an adversary to physically press the keypad buttons. Such an attack is significantly more difficult than a remote attack.
	This threat has the same threat tree as the threat of reading the speed-dial list (outlined in Table A-11) because it requires the same privileges (local call privilege for physical access; administrator privilege for remote) and is accessed in the same manner.
	Related use scenarios:
	(2) If Phone 1.0 is installed in a location where untrusted users can access it....
Investigation notes	None
Entry points	(2) Keypad
	(6) Remote administration
Assets	(1) Speed-dial list
Threat tree	None

Table A-16 Threat: Disabling the Ringer

ID	7
Name	Adversary disables the ringer
Description	If the ringer is disabled, the local user will not know when incoming calls are made.
STRIDE classification	Denial of service
Mitigated?	Yes
Known mitigation	See the table's investigation notes.
	Related use scenarios:
	(2) If Phone 1.0 is installed in a location where untrusted users can access it....
	(3) Fabrikam did not design Phone 1.0 to withstand attacks aginst the physical device....

Table A-16   Threat: Disabling the Ringer

Investigation notes	Only an administrator can disable the ringer. Gaining administrative privileges remotely is already covered in Threat 1.
	An adversary can also disable the ringer by physically opening the phone and cutting the wires leading to the loudspeaker. Because the phone application does not protect against attacks to the physical device, this is not listed as a vulnerability.
Entry points	(5) Audible ringer
Assets	(8) Alertion mechanisms
Threat tree	None

Table A-17   Threat: Conversation Snooping

ID	8
Name	Adversary intercepts a conversation
Description	The conversation between a user of Phone 1.0 and a remote user could be intercepted.
STRIDE classification	■ Information disclosure ■ Elevation of privilege
Mitigated?	Yes
Known mitigation	See the threat tree in this table. The phone was not designed to mitigate against physical attacks (such as implanting a bug), and the security of the PSTN is outside the scope of this threat model. The possible attack of an adversary who is within physical proximity of the phone and overhears a private conversation is also considered external to this threat model.
	Related use scenarios:
	(1) The Phone 1.0 will be connected to the public switched telephone network....
	(3) Fabrikam did not design Phone 1.0 to withstand attacks aginst the physical device....
Investigation notes	None
Entry points	(3) Telephone line (1) Handset
Assets	(7) Telephone conversation

Table A-17   Threat: Conversation Snooping

Threat tree

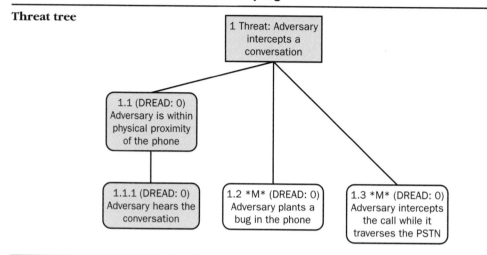

Table A-18   Threat: Message Disclosure

ID	9
Name	Adversary accesses messages
Description	Messages left by callers can contain sensitive information. Access to these messages should be granted only to local authorized users or to remote administrators via the administration interface.
STRIDE classification	Information disclosure
Mitigated?	Yes
Known mitigation	This threat has the same threat tree as the threat of an adversary reading the speed-dial list, depicted in Table A-11. Accessing the messages also requires the same privileges (local call privilege for physical access; administrative privilege for the remote administration interface) as reading the speed-dial list.
Investigation notes	Accessing the messages requires local caller privileges or better, which are granted either locally or via the remote administration interface. Accessing the messages has the same threat tree as that of reading a speed-dial list, as shown in Table A-11.
Entry points	(2) Keypad
	(1) Handset
	(6) Remote administration
	(4) Alphanumeric display
Assets	(6) Messages
Threat tree	None

Table A-19   Threat: Filling the Message Store

ID	10
Name	Adversary fills the message store
Description	A remote user could try to fill the message store so that the owner of Phone 1.0 cannot receive new messages.
STRIDE classification	Denial of service
Mitigated?	No
Known mitigation	None
Investigation notes	None
Entry points	(3) Telephone Line
Assets	(9) Message store
Threat tree	None

Table A-20   Threat: Modification of the Outgoing Greeting

ID	11
Name	Adversary modifies the outgoing message
Description	A malicious user could try to change the outgoing greeting to hurt the reputation or cause other damage to the organization using Phone 1.0.
STRIDE classification	Tampering
Mitigated?	Yes
Known mitigation	See the investigation notes in this table.
Investigation notes	The outgoing message is stored in a fixed location with a fixed size of 128 KB at the end of the 8-MB message store. To change the message, an adversary would have to gain administrative privileges locally or remotely, or she would have to somehow overwrite the buffer holding the message. Because both the outgoing message and the messages left by callers are stored in the message store, an adversary could try to fill the message store and spill over into the outgoing message buffer at the end of the store. However, because this location is fixed, Phone 1.0 employs logic to prevent writing caller messages to this area. To write to this area, the phone must be in administrative mode—meaning that administrative privileges are required to change or delete the message.

Table A-20   Threat: Modification of the Outgoing Greeting

Entry points	(1) Handset
	(2) Keypad
	(6) Remote administration
Assets	(10) Outgoing greeting
Threat tree	None

Table A-21   Threat: Deletion of Messages or Speed-Dial Entries

ID	12
Name	Adversary deletes messages and speed-dial information
Description	An attacker could try to delete messages or speed-dial information so that the owner of Phone 1.0 loses important information.
STRIDE classification	■ Tampering ■ Denial of service
Mitigated?	Yes
Known mitigation	This threat has the same threat tree as that of an adversary reading the speed-dial list, shown in Table A-11. In addition, deleting messages and speed-dial information requires the same privileges (local call privilege for physical access; administrative privilege for the remote administration interface) as reading the speed-dial list.
Investigation notes	None
Entry points	(2) Keypad
	(6) Remote administration
Assets	(1) Speed-dial list
	(6) Messages
Threat tree	None

Vulnerabilities

The known vulnerabilities of the Fabrikam Phone 1.0 system are listed in this series of tables—one table for each vulnerability. Each table includes the risk associated with not fixing the vulnerability, allowing developers to chose mitigation strategies appropriately.

Table A-22   Vulnerability: User Gains Access to the Administration Interface

ID	1
Name	A user gains access to the administration interface
Description	If the default password is left unchanged and the remote administration interface is enabled, remote anonymous users can easily obtain access to the interface.
STRIDE classification	■ Tampering ■ Information disclosure ■ Denial of service ■ Elevation of privilege
DREAD rating	7.6
Corresponding threat ID	1: Adversary gains access to the remote administration interface, resulting in access to the phone configuration
Bug	432

Table A-23   Vulnerability: Password Brute-Force Attack Against Ring Buffer

ID	2
Name	A user takes advantage of the password ring buffer
Description	If a user takes advantage of the password for the administrative interface being a ring buffer, the attack could take less than 10^8 attempts.
STRIDE classification	■ Tampering ■ Information disclosure ■ Denial of service ■ Elevation of privilege
DREAD rating	3.8
Corresponding threat ID	1: Adversary gains access to the remote administration interface, resulting in access to the phone configuration
Bug	443

Table A-24   Vulnerability: Filling the Message Store

ID	3
Name	Adversary repeatedly leaves messages on the phone, filling the message store
Description	An adversary can repeatedly call the Phone 1.0 application and leave repeated messages, thereby filling the message store. Because messages can be up to 60 seconds long, an adversary can fill the store quickly. Once the store is full, no more messages can be received.
	For mitigation, Fabrikam might add a throttling based on caller ID information that can be enabled or disabled via the administration interface.
STRIDE classification	Denial of service
DREAD rating	6.4
Corresponding threat ID	10: Adversary fills the message store
Bug	478

Appendix B

Humongous Insurance Price Quote Website

The Humongous Insurance Price Quote Website threat model presents some of the threats and issues that might be found in a Web application. This website is purposely limited in functionality to present threat modeling concepts without delving into the technology and product-specific issues that might be present in a modern Web application's threat model.

Table B-1 contains high-level information about the threat model being developed for the Price Quote Website application. This basic information includes the type of product and its location, the owner of the threat model and the team members, and any available milestone information.

Table B-1   **Threat Model Information**

Product	Price Quote Website
Milestone	Version 1.0
Owner	Darin Lockert
Participants	Don Funk, Jeffrey L. Ford, Luca Dellamore
Reviewer	Janice Galvin
Location	Humongous Insurance\Humongous Insurance Price Quote Website
Description	Humongous Insurance created an insurance price quote website to serve the needs of the company's growing online user base. This initial version of the website application has limited functionality. The application allows a user to create a profile (which includes a login and associated user data) that an insurance agent can review and use to respond with an insurance quote.

Use Scenarios

Table B-2 lists the known use scenarios for the application. This table provides information about the expected use of the application. Using or deploying the application in a way that violates a use scenario can impact the security of the application.

Table B-2   Use Scenarios

ID	Description
1	The Price Quote Website application will be installed on a Web server that has been secured to current industry guidelines. Current security patches for the Web server must be maintained.
2	The Price Quote Website will be installed on a database server that has been secured to current industry guidelines. Current security patches for the database server must be maintained.
3	The database server should be protected from direct access from the Internet by a firewall.
4	The Web server should be protected from direct access (except for the HTTP and HTTPS ports) from the Internet by a firewall.
5	Communication between the Web server and the database server should be conducted over a private network.
6	The Price Quote Website application should be deployed over HTTPS, except for the Welcome page, which might be accessible via HTTP.

External Dependencies

Table B-3 lists the external dependencies the application has on other components or products that can impact security. These dependencies are assumptions made about the usage or behavior of those other components or products. Inconsistencies can lead to security weaknesses in the Price Quote Website application.

Table B-3   External Dependencies

ID	Description
1	The Price Quote Website depends on the security of the Web server it is installed on. See Table B-2 for the corresponding use scenario.
2	The Price Quote Website depends on the security of the database server it is installed on. See Table B-2 for the corresponding use scenario.

Table B-3   External Dependencies

ID	Description
3	The Price Quote Website depends on the security of the network between the Web server and the database server. If this network is compromised, sensitive data could be viewed or direct attacks on the database server could be made.
4	The Price Quote Website depends on the session management of the Web server being secure. If the Web server's session management is not secure, an adversary might be able to hijack another user's session.
5	The Price Quote Website depends on an external Simple Mail Transfer Protocol (SMTP) server to deliver notifications of available quotes.

Implementation Assumptions

Table B-4 lists the application's implementation assumptions and describes the assumptions made about the internal workings of the component during the specification phase, but before implementation has started. These assumptions should not be violated. Typically, the threat modeling team will review them further once implementation is in place.

Table B-4   Implementation Assumptions

ID	Description
1	None. The Price Quote Website application is fully implemented.

External Security Notes

Table B-5 lists the external security notes—the threats or other information that an application user should be aware of to prevent possible vulnerabilities. These notes can include features that, if used incorrectly, could cause security problems for application users.

Table B-5   External Security Notes

ID	Description
1	The Price Quote Website application has no password quality enforcement. Users and insurance agents must choose strong passwords that are hard to guess or discover by brute force.
2	Insurance agent logins must be created directly through the database and cannot be created by the website. When creating insurance agent logins, the database administrator should ensure that communications to the database server are secure.

Internal Security Notes

Table B-6 lists the internal security notes, which contain security information that is relevant only to a person reading the threat model. These notes can be used to explain choices and design decisions that impact the product's security but were made due to overriding business needs.

Table B-6   Internal Security Notes

ID	Description
1	Because the Price Quote Website application does not use integrated authentication of any kind, end-to-end authentication and identity are not used. Supporting SQL authentication would delay the deployment of the website. In addition, the database in use supports connection pooling only when all connections use the same credentials. Thus, all queries to the database are done using one set of credentials (namely, the process identity of the Web server). Therefore, if an attack such as a SQL injection were to occur, the adversary would gain access to all tables in the database.
2	Humongous Insurance already has an SMTP server in its perimeter network (also known as the demilitarized zone or DMZ) that is used as a mail server for other Web applications. This system is controlled by another group, which is why the SMTP server is not considered in this threat model.

Trust Levels

Table B-7 lists the trust levels and describes privilege levels that are associated with entry points and assets.

Table B-7   Trust Levels

ID	Name	Description
1	Remote anonymous user	A user who has connected to the website but has not provided valid credentials yet.
2	Remote user with login credentials	A user who has created an account and has entered valid login credentials.
3	Insurance agent	Uses login credentials to view the Quote Review page.
4	Website administrator	An administrator that can configure the insurance quote website.
5	Database server administrator	An administrator that can access and modify the database and the information in it.
6	Web server process identity	Used to authenticate the Web server to the database when storing or retrieving information. All actions taken by the Web server process occur under this identity.
7	Database server process identity	The account that the database server process runs as, represented by its process token. The database process has all the access and privileges that correspond to this token.
8	HTTP user	A remote user that accesses a page via HTTP.
9	HTTPS user	A remote user that accesses a page via HTTPS.

Entry Points

Table B-8 lists the entry points and describes the interfaces through which external entities can interact with the component, either by direct interaction or by indirectly supplying it with data.

Table B-8   Entry Points

ID	Name	Description	Trust Level
1	Web server listening port (HTTPS)	The port (HTTPS) that the Web server listens on. Most of the site's Web pages are layered on this port.	(1) Remote anonymous user (2) Remote user with login credentials (3) Insurance agent (4) Website administrator (9) HTTPS user
1.1	Login page	Page for users to create a login and perform a login to the site to begin requesting or reviewing an insurance quote.	(1) Remote anonymous user (2) Remote user with login credentials (3) Insurance agent (9) HTTPS user
1.1.1	*CreateLogin* function	Creates a new user login. (Insurance agent logins must be created directly through the database stored procedures.)	(1) Remote anonymous user
1.1.2	*LoginToSite* function	Compares user-supplied credentials to those in the database and creates a new session if the credentials match.	(1) Remote anonymous user (2) Remote user with login credentials (3) Insurance agent
1.2	Data entry page	Page used to enter user's personal data into the database so that insurance agents can review it.	(2) Remote user with login credentials (9) HTTPS user
1.2.1	*RetrieveData* function	Allows the user to view his previously entered information along with the insurance quote, if available.	(2) Remote user with login credentials
1.2.2	*SubmitData* function	Submits user data to be reviewed by the insurance agent.	(2) Remote user with login credentials
1.3	Insurance agent Quote Review page	Page used by insurance agents to review a user's request for a quote. Agents also use this page to enter insurance quote information.	(3) Insurance agent (9) HTTPS user

Table B-8   Entry Points

ID	Name	Description	Trust Level
1.3.1	*RetrieveData* function	Retrieves user data so that the insurance agent can generate an insurance quote.	(3) Insurance agent
1.3.2	*SubmitData* function	Submits an insurance quote for the user to review.	(3) Insurance agent
1.3.3	*ListRequests* function	Lists quote requests ready for review.	(3) Insurance agent
2	Database listening port	Enables the database to be used remotely.	(1) Remote anonymous user (5) Database server administrator (6) Web server process identity (7) Database server process identity
2.1	Database stored procedures	Store and retrieve quote-related information in the database.	(1) Remote anonymous user (2) Remote user with login credentials (3) Insurance agent (5) Database server administrator (6) Web server process identity
2.1.1	*CreateLogin* procedure	Creates a website login for a user or an insurance agent.	(1) Remote anonymous user (5) Database server administrator (6) Web server process identity
2.1.2	*RemoveLogin* procedure	Removes a login, including any user data, if the login is a user rather than an insurance agent.	(5) Database server administrator (6) Web server process identity

Table B-8 Entry Points

ID	Name	Description	Trust Level
2.1.3	*StoreUserData* procedure	Used to store user data from the data entry page of the website.	(2) Remote user with login credentials (5) Database server administrator (6) Web server process identity
2.1.4	*RetrieveUserData* procedure	Retrieves the user's data and insurance quote.	(2) Remote user with login credentials (3) Insurance agent (5) Database server administrator (6) Web server process identity
2.1.5	*StoreQuoteData* procedure	Used by the insurance agent Quote Review page to store an insurance quote for the user to view.	(3) Insurance agent (5) Database server administrator (6) Web server process identity
2.1.6	*RetrieveCredentials* procedure	Used to retrieve login credentials for a user or insurance agent. The website compares this information to the credentials that the user sends to the login page.	(5) Database server administrator (6) Web server process identity
3	Web pages from disk	The Web pages on disk are entry points. The Web server reads these files and uses the code in them to process requests.	(4) Website administrator (6) Web server process identity
4	Web server listening port (HTTP)	The HTTP port that the Web server listens on. Only the Welcome page is layered on this port.	(1) Remote anonymous user (8) HTTP user
4.1	Welcome page	A static HTML page that informs the user about the Price Quote Website and redirects him to the login page.	(1) Remote anonymous user (8) HTTP user
5	Connection to SMTP server	The Price Quote Website connects to an SMTP server to send notification e-mails.	(6) Web server process identity

Assets

Table B-9 lists the assets and describes the data or functionality that the component needs to protect. This table also lists the minimum access category (trust level) that should be allowed to access the resource.

Table B-9   Assets

ID	Name	Description	Trust Level
13	User and agent	Assets that relate to a user or insurance agent.	
13.1	User's login data	The user's credentials: username and password.	(2) Remote user with login credentials (5) Database server administrator
13.7	Insurance agent's login data	The insurance agent's credentials: username and password.	(3) Insurance agent (5) Database server administrator
13.2	User's personal data	The personal data that the user enters, such as contact information and assets.	(2) Remote user with login credentials (3) Insurance agent
14	System	Assets that relate to the underlying system.	
14.12	Availability of the site	If the Price Quote Website goes down, users cannot request or receive quotes.	(4) Website administrator (5) Database server administrator
15	Process	Assets that relate to the process running the website.	
15.4	Ability to execute code as the identity of the Web server	Web pages on the site execute code by using the security token of the Web server.	(4) Website administrator (6) Web server process identity
15.5	Ability to execute code as the identity of the database server	Database queries and procedures execute code using the security token of the database server.	(5) Database server administrator (7) Database server process identity
16	Application	Assets that relate to the Web application.	

Table B-9 **Assets**

ID	Name	Description	Trust Level
16.8	Login session	The Web session associated with a logged-in user or insurance agent.	(2) Remote user with login credentials (3) Insurance agent
16.3	Access to backend database	The ability to interact with the database that stores user data, insurance quotes, and login credentials.	(5) Database server administrator (6) Web server process identity (7) Database server process identity
16.6	Accuracy of the price quote	The insurance price quote must be accurate. An adversary tampering with this quote could cause loss of business.	(3) Insurance agent
16.9	Access to the insurance agent pages	Only insurance agents should be able to view the insurance agent pages.	(3) Insurance agent
16.10	E-mail notification of ready quote	The e-mail notification lets the user know when a quote is ready.	(2) Remote user with login credentials (3) Insurance agent
16.11	Notification of new quote request	Only quote requests in the notify list will be seen by insurance agents.	(2) Remote user with login credentials (3) Insurance agent
16.1	Audit data	Adversaries might try to attack the system without being logged or audited.	(4) Website administrator (5) Database server administrator (6) Web server process identity (7) Database server process identity

Data Flow Diagrams

Figure B-1 shows the context-level data flow diagram (DFD) for the Humongous Insurance Price Quote Website application. The system is represented as two processing nodes to denote a computer boundary. Users, agents, and servers external to the website are shown as external entities.

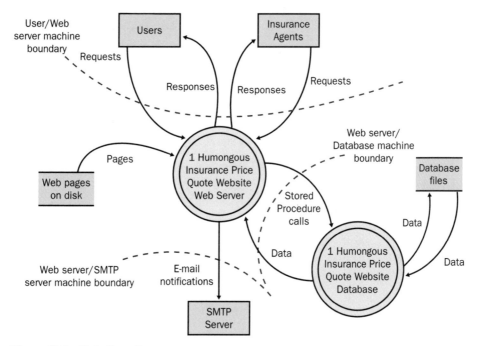

Figure B-1   Data flow diagram.

Threats

The threats to the application are listed in a series of tables—one for each threat. These threats do not imply vulnerabilities. Rather, they are actions that a malicious external entity might try to perform to exploit the system.

Table B-10   Threat: Malicious SQL Data in User Input

ID	1
Name	Adversary supplies malicious data in a request targeting the SQL command-parsing engine in an attempt to change execution
Description	An adversary might try to inject SQL commands into the application via data she supplies, such as her login name or personal information. If this data is not handled properly by the Price Quote Website, this could result in SQL injection. In addition, other malicious input could cause the system to become unstable or leak information.
STRIDE classification	■ Tampering ■ Elevation of privilege
Mitigated?	No

Table B-10   Threat: Malicious SQL Data in User Input

Known mitigation	None
Investigation notes	The database stored procedures were code reviewed for any use of string concatenation in freeform EXEC queries. The *RetrieveCredentials* stored procedure was the only procedure with this error. The procedure concatenates the *@username* parameter to a SELECT statement:
	`EXEC('SELECT Password FROM LoginTable WHERE Username = ' + @username)`
	Because the *@username* parameter is not validated, an attacker could supply a malicious string that, when concatenated with the rest of the statement and then reparsed by the SQL server, could result in arbitrary queries being run.
Entry points	(1.1) Login page
	(1.2) Data entry page
	(1.3) Insurance agent Quote Review page
Assets	(16.3) Access to backend database
Threat tree	None

Table B-11   Threat: Disclosure of Login Information

ID	2
Name	Adversary acquires the username and password or another user or agent
Description	If an adversary obtains the login credentials of another user or agent, he can do perform any task that user can.
STRIDE classification	■ Information disclosure
	■ Elevation of privilege
Mitigated?	No
Known mitigation	*Related use scenarios:*
	(3) The database server should be protected from direct access from the Internet by a firewall.
	Related external security notes:
	(1) No password quality enforcement exists in the Price Quote Website. It is up to users and agents to choose strong passwords that are hard to guess or brute-force discover.
Investigation notes	None
Entry points	(1.1) Login page
	(2.1) Database stored procedures

Table B-11   Threat: Disclosure of Login Information

Assets   (13.1) User's login data

                    (13.7) Insurance agent's login data

Threat tree

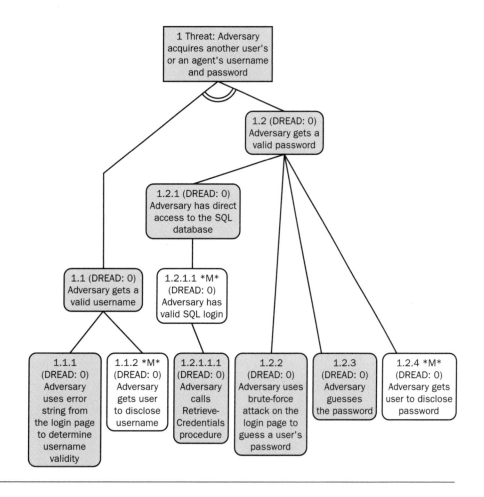

Table B-12   **Threat: Session ID Theft**

ID	3
Name	Adversary acquires the session ID of another user or agent
Description	If an attacker acquires the session ID of a logged-in user or agent, she can perform any task that user can.
STRIDE classification	Elevation of privilege
Mitigated?	Yes
Known mitigation	The Price Quote Website depends on the cryptographic security of the Web server's session management. In addition, the session is established only after the user accesses the login page. Because this should be done over the Secure Socket Layer (SSL), an adversary should not be able to snoop the session identifier. (For more information, see the mitigating use scenario below.)
	Related use scenarios:
	(6) The Price Quote Website should be deployed over HTTPS, except for the Welcome page, which may accessible via HTTP.
	Related external dependencies:
	(4) The Price Quote Website depends on the session management of the Web server to be secure. If it is not, an adversary might be able to hijack another user's session.
Investigation notes	None
Entry points	(1) Web server listening port (HTTPS)
Assets	(16.8) Login session
Threat tree	None

Table B-13   **Threat: User Data Disclosure**

ID	4
Name	Adversary retrieves another user's personal data
Description	Disclosing another user's personal data raises privacy issues. Furthermore, Humongous Insurance would not be perceived as trustworthy.
STRIDE classification	■ Spoofing ■ Information disclosure
Mitigated?	No
Known mitigation	None

Table B-13   Threat: User Data Disclosure

Investigation notes	None
Entry points	(1.2) Data entry page
	(2.1) Database stored procedures
Assets	(13.2) User's personal data
Threat tree	

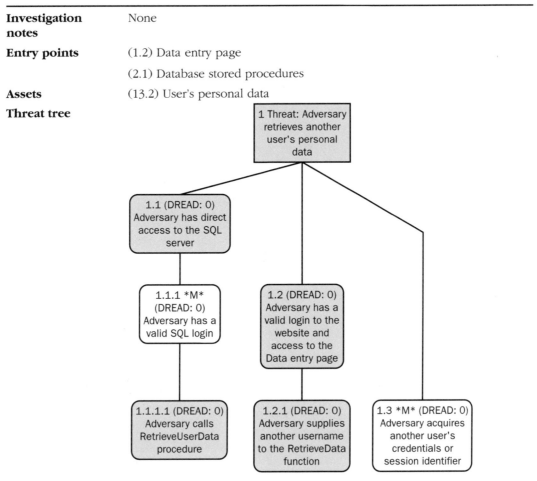

Table B-14   Threat: Direct Access to the Database

ID	5
Name	Adversary accesses the backend database directly
Description	An adversary who can access the backend database directly might be able to tamper with or view the data stored in it, including account names and passwords.
STRIDE classification	■ Tampering
	■ Repudiation
	■ Information disclosure
	■ Elevation of privilege

Table B-14   Threat: Direct Access to the Database

Mitigated?	Yes
Known mitigation	For this to be a vulnerability, the website would have to be deployed in an unsupported configuration or an adversary would have to be able to execute code on the Web server, which has network access to the database.
	Related use scenarios:
	(3) The database server should be protected from direct access from the Internet by a firewall.
	(5) Communication between the Web server and the database server should be over a private network.
Investigation notes	None
Entry points	(2) Database listening port
Assets	(13.1) User's login data
	(13.7) Insurance agent's login data
	(13.2) User's personal data
	(16.6) Accuracy of the price quote
Threat tree	None

Table B-15   Threat: Rate Quote Tampering

ID	6
Name	Adversary modifies a user's price quote
Description	An adversary who wants to damage Humongous Insurance's business might try to modify price quotes so that they are always higher than those of competitors.
STRIDE classification	Tampering
Mitigated?	Yes
Known mitigation	See corresponding threat tree in this table.
Investigation notes	None
Entry points	(1.3) Insurance agent Quote Review page
	(2.1) Database stored procedures
Assets	(16.6) Accuracy of the price quote

Table B-15   Threat: Rate Quote Tampering

Threat tree

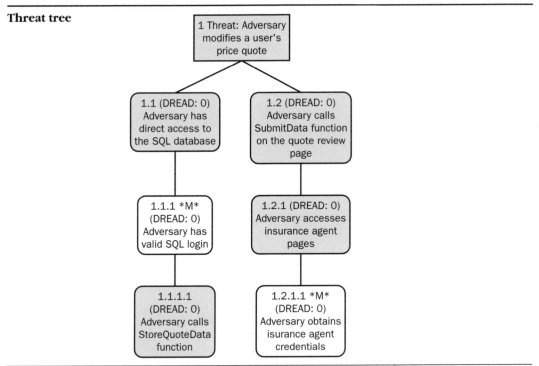

Table B-16   Threat: Unauthorized Use of Insurance Agent Web Pages

ID	7
Name	Adversary accesses insurance agent Web pages
Description	An adversary who can access the insurance agent Web pages might be able to view sensitive information.
STRIDE classification	Elevation of privilege
Mitigated?	Yes
Known mitigation	The insurance agent Web pages check server-side session state to determine whether the user associated with the session is an insurance agent. If the user is not an agent, the user is redirected to the login page.

Table B-16 Threat: Unauthorized Use of Insurance Agent Web Pages

Investigation notes	None
Entry points	(1.3) Insurance agent Quote Review page
Assets	(16.9) Access to the insurance agent Web pages
Threat tree	None

Table B-17 Threat: Blocking E-Mail Notifications

ID	8
Name	Adversary prevents a user from receiving e-mail notification of an available quote
Description	If the user does not receive the e-mail notification of the available quote, she might not pursue buying an insurance policy from Humongous Insurance.
STRIDE classification	Denial of service
Mitigated?	Yes
Known mitigation	The e-mail server is external to the Price Quote Website application. The security of that server is controlled by another group. If the website cannot contact the Web server, the site will queue the notification and try resending the e-mail at recurring, configurable time intervals.
	Related external dependencies:
	(5) The Price Quote Website depends on an external SMTP server to deliver notifications of ready quotes.
Investigation notes	None
Entry points	(5) Connection to SMTP server
Assets	(16.10) E-mail notification of available quote
Threat tree	None

Table B-18   Threat: Blocking New Quote Request Notifications

ID	9
Name	Adversary prevents insurance agents from receiving notification of new quote requests
Description	If the insurance agent does not receive notification that new requests are waiting, those requests will not be processed.
STRIDE classification	Denial of service
Mitigated?	Yes
Known mitigation	See corresponding investigation notes in this table.
Investigation notes	The list of quote requests is retrieved when an insurance agent logs in. No methods of blocking this list were found.
Entry points	(1.3) Insurance agent Quote Review page
	(2.1) Database stored procedures
Assets	(16.11) Notification of new quote request
Threat tree	None

Table B-19   Threat: User Data Tampering

ID	10
Name	Adversary modifies another user's personal data
Description	Modifying another user's data could alter that user's quoted price and would make Humongous Insurance look untrustworthy.
STRIDE classification	■ Spoofing ■ Tampering ■ Elevation of privilege
Mitigated?	No
Known mitigation	None
Investigation notes	See the threat tree in Table B-13—specifically, the threat of retrieving another user's personal data.
Entry points	(1.2) Data entry page
	(2.1) Database stored procedures
Assets	(13.2) User's personal data
Threat tree	None

Table B-20   **Threat: Account Deletion**

ID	11
Name	Adversary deletes a user or agent account
Description	This deletion of a user or agent account would cause a denial of service. The user or agent would no longer be able to work with the Price Quote Website.
STRIDE classification	■ Denial of service ■ Elevation of privilege
Mitigated?	Yes
Known mitigation	See the corresponding mitigation use scenarios below. *Related use scenarios:* (3) The database server should be protected from direct access from the Internet by a firewall. (5) Communication between the Web server and the database server should be over a private network.
Investigation notes	The website does not support deleting accounts directly. This must be done by connecting directly to the database and calling the *RemoveLogin* procedure.
Entry points	(2.1) Database stored procedures
Assets	(13.1) User's login data (13.7) Insurance agent's login data
Threat tree	None

Table B-21   **Threat: Crashing the Website**

ID	12
Name	Adversary crashes the Price Quote Website
Description	Crashing the website would cause a denial of service, preventing quotes from being requested or reviewed.
STRIDE classification	Denial of service
Mitigated?	Yes

Table B-21   **Threat: Crashing the Website**

Known mitigation	Stress testing the website is part of the test suite. In addition, the test suite has numerous invalid input tests to ensure the website can handle malformed data.
	Related use scenarios:
	(1) The Price Quote Website will be installed on a Web server that has been secured to current industry guidelines. Current security patches for the Web server must be maintained.
Investigation notes	None
Entry points	(1) Web server listening port (HTTPS)
	(2) Database listening port
	(4) Web server listening port (HTTP)
Assets	(14.12) Availability of the site
Threat tree	None

Table B-22   **Threat: Accessing the Site Without Valid Credentials**

ID	13
Name	Adversary without valid credentials accesses the site
Description	An adversary without any credentials might try to access a user's account or the insurance agent Web pages.
STRIDE classification	Elevation of privilege
Mitigated?	Yes
Known mitigation	All pages redirect to the login page if the server-side session state does not indicate a logged-in session. A session is marked as logged in only if the user-supplied password matches that in the database.
	Related external dependencies:
	(4) The Price Quote Website depends on the session management of the Web server to be secure. If it is not, an adversary might be able to hijack another user's session.
Investigation notes	None
Entry points	(1.1) Login page
	(1.2) Data entry page
	(1.3) Insurance agent Quote Review page
Assets	(13.2) User's personal data
Threat tree	None

Table B-23   Threat: Intercepting Available Quote Notification

ID	14
Name	Adversary intercepts e-mail notification of available quote
Description	The adversary would be able to view any sensitive data in the email.
STRIDE classification	Information disclosure
Mitigated?	Yes
Known mitigation	The information in the e-mail consists of the username and a message stating that the quote is ready. The e-mail message does not contain quote information or personal data. Thus, even if the message is intercepted, no sensitive data will be disclosed.
Investigation notes	None
Entry points	(5) Connection to SMTP server
Assets	(16.10) E-mail notification of available quote
Threat tree	None

Table B-24   Threat: Access Without Auditing

ID	15
Name	Adversary tries to access another user's data without being logged
Description	If no logging occurs, there is no way of knowing that the attack occurred and no evidence to indicate where the attack came from.
STRIDE classification	Repudiation
Mitigated?	No
Known mitigation	None
Investigation notes	Other than minimal built-in Web server logging, the website has no logging.
Entry points	(1.2) Data entry page
Assets	(16.1) Audit data
Threat tree	None

Vulnerabilities

The known vulnerabilities to the system are listed in a series of tables in this section—one table for each vulnerability. Each table includes the risk associated with not fixing the vulnerability so that threat modeling teams can choose mitigation strategies appropriately.

Table B-25   Vulnerability: SQL Injection

ID	1
Name	*RetrieveCredentials* SQL injection
Description	The *RetrieveCredentials* procedure concatenates the *@username* parameter to a SELECT statement:
	`EXEC('SELECT Password FROM LoginTable WHERE Username = ' + @username)`
	Because the *@username* parameter is not validated, an attacker could supply a malicious string that, when concatenated with the rest of the statement and then reparsed by the instance of SQL Server, could result in arbitrary queries being run. The *@username* parameter should be sanitized for malicious input, or a parameterized version should be used.
STRIDE classification	■ Tampering ■ Elevation of privilege
DREAD rating	10
Corresponding threat ID	1: Adversary uses special SQL characters or keywords in her input to attempt to execute code on the database server
Bug	223

Table B-26   Vulnerability: Username Discoverability

ID	2
Name	Confirmation of whether a username exists via login page error strings
Description	The login page returns two errors, "Bad username" and "Bad password." These errors allow an adversary to determine whether a username exists. Damage potential is low because this information alone does not grant the adversary access to the website application; the adversary still has to guess the password. In addition, exploitability is low because the adversary must guess the username as well.
STRIDE classification	■ Information disclosure ■ Elevation of privilege
DREAD rating	6.6
Corresponding threat ID	2: Adversary acquires the username and password or another user or agent
Bug	250

Table B-27 Vulnerability User Data Disclosure

ID	3
Name	User data disclosure in the *RetrieveData* function on the data entry page
Description	The *RetrieveData* function on the data entry page uses a parameter in the HTTP request (username) to determine which user's data to retrieve from the database. The username should instead be retrieved from server-side session state so that the client cannot arbitrarily supply the username.
STRIDE classification	■ Spoofing ■ Information disclosure
DREAD rating	9.2
Corresponding threat ID	4: Adversary retrieves another user's personal data
Bug	251

Table B-28 Vulnerability: Data Tampering

ID	4
Name	User tampers with data in the *SubmitData* function on the data entry page
Description	The *SubmitData* function on the data entry page uses a parameter in the HTTP request (username) to determine which user's data to store to the database. The username should instead be retrieved from server-side session state so that the client cannot arbitrarily supply the username.
STRIDE classification	■ Spoofing ■ Tampering ■ Elevation of privilege
DREAD rating	9.2
Corresponding Threat ID	10: Adversary modifies another user's personal data
Bug	259

Table B-29   Vulnerability: Nonexistent Logging and Auditing

ID	5
Name	The Price Quote Website has no logging or auditing
Description	Humongous Insurance needs to determine what functionality should be logged and audited. The company must also assess the legal ramifications of this.
STRIDE classification	Repudiation
DREAD rating	5.2
Corresponding threat ID	15: Adversary tries to access other user's data without being logged
Bug	260

Appendix C

A. Datum Access Control API

The A. Datum Access Control API threat model illustrates how threat modeling can be applied to a software library that is used by other applications. A. Datum's Access Control API might be integrated into any application that needs to protect user and group access to resources. This example shows how threat modeling can be performed at the software feature level. In this case, the feature is the access control class library.

Table C-1 contains the high-level information about the threat model being developed for the A. Datum Access Control API application. This basic information includes the type of product and its location, the owner of the threat model and team members, and any available milestone information.

Table C-1   Threat Model Information

Product	Access Control API
Milestone	RTM
Owner	Ann Beebe
Participants	Kari Hensien, Magnus Hedlund, Scott Gode
Reviewer	Bradley Beck
Location	A. Datum Libraries\A. Datum Access Control API
Description	The A. Datum Access Control API is a class library that can be used by application developers to protect user and group access to resources. The class library has an abstracted concept of a hierarchical resource tree that can have access control lists applied on a resource-by-resource basis. Library users must supply a class that maps this resource tree to the underlying resources being protected. Access control lists are inherited from the parent unless otherwise specified. The library can also implicitly generate resource nodes if Implicit mode is set.

Use Scenarios

Table C-2 lists the use scenarios for the application—in other words, information about its expected use. Using or deploying the application in a way that violates these use scenarios can impact the security of the component.

Table C-2   Use Scenarios

ID	Description
1	*ACADatumOSFilePathResolver* is an implementation of *IACPathResolver* that resolves pathnames on A. Datum Operating System 1.0 but will not work for other operating systems. Using this implementation on other operating systems could result in incorrectly mapping pathnames to the A. Datum Access Control API canonical form.

External Dependencies

Table C-3 lists the external dependencies on other components or products that can impact the Access Control API's security. These dependencies are assumptions made about the usage or behavior of those other components or products. Inconsistencies in these assumptions can lead to security weaknesses in the API.

Table C-3   External Dependencies

ID	Description
1	The *ACADatumOSFilePathResolver* depends on file paths in A. Datum Operating System 1.0 being resolved in the same manner as implemented in this class. If the file paths resolve differently in the operating system, the mapping that the *ACADatumOSFilePathResolver* performs could result in an incorrect resource being checked for access. At worst, this could allow an adversary to access a file he could not normally access.

Implementation Assumptions

Table C-4 describes the implementation assumptions made about the internal workings of the component during the specification phase, but before implementation has started. These assumptions should not be violated. Typically, the threat modeling team will further review these assumptions once implementation is in place.

Table C-4 **Implementation Assumptions**

ID	Description
1	If Deny is added to the Access Control API, any Deny should have precedence over any Allow. Thus, if a user is denied access to a resource or the user belongs to a group that is denied access, the denial of access takes precedence over any Allow granted to the user or a group she belongs to.

External Security Notes

Table C-5 lists the external security notes—the information that an application user should be aware of to prevent possible vulnerabilities. These notes can include features that, if used incorrectly, could cause security problems for application users.

Table C-5 **External Security Notes**

ID	Description
1	*ACADatumOSFilePathResolver* is intended for use on A. Datum's Operating System 1.0 only. Using *ACADatumOSFilePathResolver* on other platforms is not supported and could cause errors.
2	Implicit mode in the *ACResources* class allows implicitly generated resources. If enabled, the *ACResources* class will generate resource nodes according to the documentation for *ACResources.SetExplicitMode*. Users who want only explicit resources to be resolved should not use Implicit mode. Furthermore, enabling Implicit mode could generate nodes for resources that do not actually exist. This is because the Access Control API does not actually reference the underlying system when generating these nodes.
3	Requesting access to a resource with no flags set will always return access granted. (Flag settings are *FlagRead* = 1, *FlagWrite* = 2, *FlagReadWrite* = 3.) Because no access rights were requested, this result is considered correct behavior. However, programmers using the API should be aware of this case and ensure that they use it appropriately.
4	Users who implement the *IACPathResolver* interface should use the same parsing and normalization as the underlying system that stores the resource. This will prevent inconsistencies between path resolution in the resolver and the underlying system, which could result in access checks being done on one resource in the Access Control API and another resource being opened by the underlying system.

Internal Security Notes

Table C-6 lists the internal security notes, which contain security information relevant only to people reading the threat model. These notes can be used to explain choices and design decisions that impact security but were made for overriding business needs.

Table C-6   Internal Security Notes

ID	Description
1	To prevent a user from causing a denial of service when Explicit mode is disabled by repeatedly requesting resources that do not exist, the implicitly generated resource nodes are not stored in the *ACResources* tree. Rather, they are created and given back to the caller who is expected to free the *ACResource* instance after using it. This helps mitigate an out-of-memory condition but comes at the cost of having to re-create implicit nodes on each request.

Trust Levels

Table C-7 lists the trust levels and describes privilege levels that are associated with application entry points and assets.

Table C-7   Trust Levels

ID	Name	Description
1	The program using the API	The process identity of the program that uses the library is the direct user of the API.
2	A user with unknown access to a resource	The process using the library passes a user's request for access to resources to the API. The user might have unknown access to the resource.
3	A user with read access to a resource	The process using the library passes a user's request for access to resources to the API. The user might have read access to the resource.
4	A user with write access to a resource	The process using the library passes a user's request for access to resources to the API. The user might have write access to the resource.

Entry Points

Table C-8 lists the entry points and describes the interfaces through which external entities can interact with the component, either via direct interaction or by indirectly supplying the component with data.

Table C-8   Entry Points

ID	Name	Description	Trust Level
1	*ACResources*	A class that represents a tree of resources. Child resource nodes in the tree inherit the access control list of their parent by default.	(1) The program using the API (2) A user with unknown access to a resource (3) A user with read access to a resource (4) A user with write access to a resource
1.1	*Add*	Adds a resource to the tree at the specified path.	(1) The program using the API
1.2	*Remove*	Removes the resource at the specified path.	(1) The program using the API
1.3	*Get*	Returns the resource at the specified path.	(1) The program using the API (2) A user with unknown access to a resource (3) A user with read access to a resource (4) A user with write access to a resource
1.4	*GetRoot*	Gets the root resource.	(1) The program using the API
1.5	*GetChildren*	Gets the child resources at the specified path.	(1) The program using the API
1.6	*GetParent*	Gets the parent resource of the specified path.	(1) The program using the API

Table C-8   **Entry Points**

ID	Name	Description	Trust Level
1.7	*SetImplicitMode*	Determines whether Implicit mode is used. If Implicit mode is disabled (in other words, if Explicit mode is used), only resources explicitly added to the tree will be used. If Implicit mode is enabled, the class will interpolate resources and automatically generate resource instances that have the access control list of their closest ancestor. For example, in Implicit mode, a user can add the following nodes: \Node1 \Node1\SubNode1\SubNode2 The collection will autogenerate the SubNode1 node with the access control list of Node1. In addition, if the user requests a resource such as \Node1\SubNode1\SubNode2 \SubNode3, the class will autogenerate SubNode3 with the access control list of SubNode2.	(1) The program using the API
1.8	*SetPathResolver*	Sets an optional path resolver that maps paths supplied to the class from an arbitrary form to the normalized form used by the *ACResources* class.	(1) The program using the API
2	*ACResource*	A resource that can have an access control list applied to it.	(1) The program using the API
2.1	*GetAcl*	Gets the access control list for the resource.	(1) The program using the API
2.2	*SetAcl*	Sets the access control list for the resource.	(1) The program using the API
3	*ACGroups*	A class that represents all groups of users. Resources can be restricted by groups, users, or both.	(1) The program using the API
3.1	*Add*	Adds a group to the list.	(1) The program using the API
3.2	*Get*	Gets a group from the list.	(1) The program using the API
3.3	*Remove*	Removes a group from the list.	(1) The program using the API

Table C-8 **Entry Points**

ID	Name	Description	Trust Level
4	*ACGroup*	A group of users. This class is used to simplify applying access control to a resource by grouping users with the same access rights.	(1) The program using the API
4.1	*AddMember*	Adds a user to the group.	(1) The program using the API
4.2	*GetMembers*	Returns a list of users in the group.	(1) The program using the API
4.3	*RemoveMember*	Removes a user from the group.	(1) The program using the API
5	*ACUsers*	A class that represents all users.	(1) The program using the API
			(2) A user with unknown access to a resource
			(3) A user with read access to a resource
			(4) A user with write access to a resource
5.1	*Add*	Adds a user to the list of users.	(1) The program using the API
5.2	*Get*	Retrieves a user based on login name.	(1) The program using the API
			(2) A user with unknown access to a resource
			(3) A user with read access to a resource
			(4) A user with write access to a resource
5.3	*Remove*	Removes a user from the list.	(1) The program using the API
6	*ACUser*	A user that can be granted access to a resource.	(1) The program using the API
6.1	*GetGroup-Membership*	Returns a list of groups the user belongs to.	(1) The program using the API
7	*ACCheck*	A class with static members that will return the access rights for a user on a specified resource.	(1) The program using the API
			(2) A user with unknown access to a resource
			(3) A user with read access to a resource
			(4) A user with write access to a resource

Table C-8 **Entry Points**

ID	Name	Description	Trust Level
7.1	*CheckAccess*	Determines whether a user has read or write access to the specified resource.	(1) The program using the API
			(2) A user with unknown access to a resource
			(3) A user with read access to a resource
			(4) A user with write access to a resource
8	*IACPathResolver*	An interface that normalizes a given string to its canonical form so that the *ACResources* class can map arbitrary string-based paths to its internal resource path.	(1) The program using the API
			(2) A user with unknown access to a resource
			(3) A user with read access to a resource
			(4) A user with write access to a resource
8.1	*Resolve*	Takes a string path and returns a normalized string path in the form that is used by the *ACResources* class.	(1) The program using the API
			(2) A user with unknown access to a resource
			(3) A user with read access to a resource
			(4) A user with write access to a resource
8.2	*ACADatumOS-FilePathResolver*	A class that translates file paths on A. Datum Operating System 1.0 to the *ACResources* normalized resource path.	(1) The program using the API
			(2) A user with unknown access to a resource
			(3) A user with read access to a resource
			(4) A user with write access to a resource
8.2.1	*Resolve*	Takes a string path of the specified file and returns a normalized string path in the form that is used by the *ACResources* class.	(1) The program using the API
			(2) A user with unknown access to a resource
			(3) A user with read access to a resource
			(4) A user with write access to a resource
9	*ACAcl*	Represents the access control list for a resource.	(1) The program using the API

Table C-8 **Entry Points**

ID	Name	Description	Trust Level
9.1	*AddGroup*	Adds a group with read and/or write access.	(1) The program using the API
9.2	*AddUser*	Adds a user with read and/or write access.	(1) The program using the API
9.3	*RemoveGroup*	Removes a group.	(1) The program using the API
9.4	*RemoveUser*	Removes a user.	(1) The program using the API
9.5	*GetGroups*	Gets the groups with access.	(1) The program using the API
9.6	*GetUsers*	Gets the users with access.	(1) The program using the API
9.7	*CheckGroup-Access*	Checks whether a group has read or write access.	(1) The program using the API
9.8	*CheckUser-Access*	Checks whether a user has read or write access.	(1) The program using the API

Assets

Table C-9 describes the data or functionality—the assets—that the component needs to protect. The table lists the minimum access category (or trust level) that should be granted access to the resource.

Table C-9 **Assets**

ID	Name	Description	Trust Level
8	Process	Assets that relate to the process that the library is running in.	None
8.6	Ability to execute arbitrary code as the identity of the process	The library executes in the process space of the program using it. Buffer overflows and similar implementation issues in the library could allow a user to execute arbitrary code.	(1) The program using the API
8.1	Availability	The access control library should not cause performance degradation to the process. Additionally, users should not be able to crash the process through the access control library.	(1) The program using the API
9	Library	Assets that relate specifically to the library.	None
9.1	Read access to resources	The ability to read from a resource.	(3) A user with read access to a resource

Table C-9 **Assets**

ID	Name	Description	Trust Level
9.2	Write access to resources	The ability to write to a resource.	(4) A user with write access to a resource
9.3	Group membership	A user in a group is granted the access that the group is granted.	(1) The program using the API
9.4	ACL entries for resources	Access control lists are used to define access for a resource. They should not be tampered with.	(1) The program using the API
9.5	Accuracy of the normalized resource path	The path must be normalized in the same way that it is normalized by any underlying system, such as the file system.	(1) The program using the API
9.6	Path discovery	A user who does not have access to a resource should not be able to determine whether that resource exists in the resource tree.	(3) A user with read access to a resource (4) A user with write access to a resource
9.7	Audit data	Knowing who attempts to access a resource is important to track both legitimate and illegitimate use.	(1) The program using the API

Data Flow Diagrams

The A. Datum Access Control API application uses two data flow diagrams (DFDs) in its threat model. Figure C-1 shows the context diagram, and Figure C-2 shows the Level 0 diagram. The context diagram shows the library being used by an application. The Level 0 diagram shows the data flow for an access check on a resource.

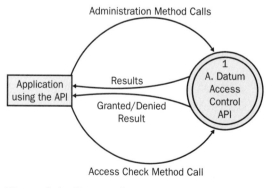

Figure C-1 Context diagram.

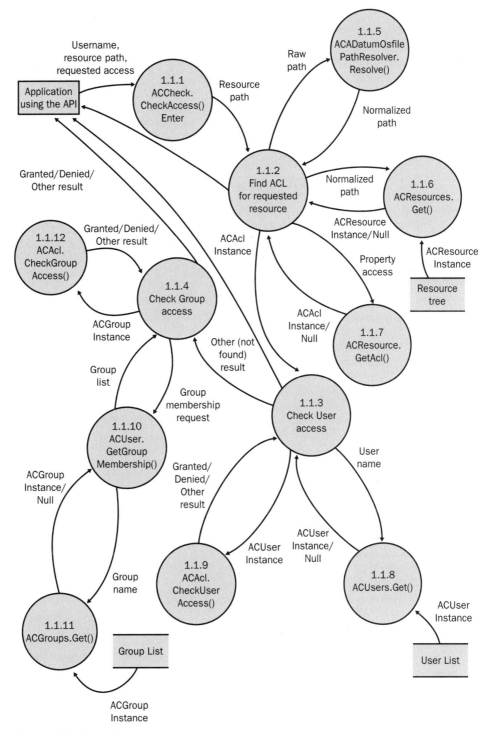

Figure C-2 Level 0 diagram.

Threats

The threats to the application are listed in this section in a series of tables—one table for each threat. These threats do not imply vulnerabilities. Rather, they are actions that a malicious external entity might try to perform to exploit the system.

Table C-10   Threat: Gaining Write Access

ID	1
Name	Adversary gains write access to a resource that he only has read access to
Description	A user with read access can try to write to the resource, changing data that he should not be able to change.
STRIDE classification	■ Tampering ■ Elevation of privilege
Mitigated?	Yes
Known mitigation	See corresponding investigation notes on how access rights are checked. Related external security notes: (3) Requesting access to a resource with no flags set....
Investigation notes	Read or write access are flags passed in the call to *ACCheck.CheckAccess*. These flags are passed to calls to *ACAcl.CheckGroupAccess* and *ACAcl.CheckUserAccess*. The algorithm for testing access is as follows (where a read flag is 1, write flag is 2, and read/write is 3):

```
boolean AccessResult = !(AccessFlags & ~(GrantedFlags));
```

This results in the following table of possibilities:

```
AccessFlags = 0, GrantedFlags = 0, Result = true
AccessFlags = 1, GrantedFlags = 0, Result = false
AccessFlags = 2, GrantedFlags = 0, Result = false
AccessFlags = 3, GrantedFlags = 0, Result = false

AccessFlags = 0, GrantedFlags = 1, Result = true
AccessFlags = 1, GrantedFlags = 1, Result = true
AccessFlags = 2, GrantedFlags = 1, Result = false
AccessFlags = 3, GrantedFlags = 1, Result = false

AccessFlags = 0, GrantedFlags = 2, Result = true
AccessFlags = 1, GrantedFlags = 2, Result = false
AccessFlags = 2, GrantedFlags = 2, Result = true
AccessFlags = 3, GrantedFlags = 2, Result = false

AccessFlags = 0, GrantedFlags = 3, Result = true
AccessFlags = 1, GrantedFlags = 3, Result = true
AccessFlags = 2, GrantedFlags = 3, Result = true
AccessFlags = 3, GrantedFlags = 3, Result = true
```

This table shows that the check for positive access is sufficient. For more details, see the threat of an adversary with a Deny gaining access to resources (Threat 11, outlined in Table C-19).

Furthermore, the calling application must ensure that it does not grant access to a resource that was not checked through a call to *ACCheck.CheckAccess*. Callers should ensure that when they open the resource, they open it using only the access flags that were checked in the call to *ACCheck.CheckAccess*.

Table C-10   **Threat: Gaining Write Access**

Entry points	(9) *ACAcl*
Assets	(9.2) Write access to resources
Threat Tree	None

Table C-11   **Threat: Malformed Path Data**

ID	2
Name	Adversary supplies malicious or malformed data as a path to the library, targeting the path parsing code
Description	An attacker could use malicious input such as long resource paths in an attempt to overflow a character buffer or integer length field.
STRIDE classification	Elevation of privilege
Mitigated?	No
Known mitigation	None
Investigation notes	A code review of *ACADatumOSFilePathResolver.Resolve* found that the buffer allocated for the file path that is passed in did not include space for a terminating (null) character. Because of allocation alignment, this omission was not caught during testing. However, if a path with a length that is a multiple of the alignment is provided (8 bytes on A. Datum Operating System 1.0), when copied to the buffer, that path will overwrite one character's worth of memory adjacent to the buffer with a null character.
	Furthermore, the path length is calculated by using an unsigned short integer (16 bits). This means that a path longer than 64 k will cause integer rollover so that the calculated length will actually be:
	ActualLength MOD 65536
	Thus, for an actual length of 65,537 characters, only 1 character will be allocated. When the path is copied, arbitrary memory beyond the one-character allocation will be overwritten with the input path.
Entry points	(8) *IACPathResolver*
	(8.2) *ACADatumOSFilePathResolver*
	(1) *ACResources*
Assets	(8.6) Ability to execute arbitrary code as the identity of the process
Threat tree	None

Table C-12 Threat: Path Normalization Attack

ID	3
Name	Adversary supplies a path that normalizes incorrectly, allowing access to an incorrect resource
Description	If a malicious user finds a discrepancy in the way the implementation of *IACPathResolver* normalizes paths compared to the underlying system, she might be able to trick the Access Control API into granting her access.
STRIDE classification	Elevation of privilege
Mitigated?	Yes
Known mitigation	The path normalization for the supplied *ACADatumOSFilePathResolver* is directly copied from AC Datum Operating System 1.0. These routines are kept in sync. For other mitigations, see the mitigating external security notes in this table.
	Related use scenarios:
	(1) *ACADatumOSFilePathResolver* is an implementation of *IACPathResolver* that resolves path names on A. Datum Operating System 1.0; it will not work for other operating systems. Using it on other operating systems could result in incorrect mapping of path names to the A. Datum Access Control API canonical form.
	Related external dependencies:
	(1) The *ACADatumOSFilePathResolver* depends on file paths in A. Datum Operating System 1.0 to be resolved in the same manner as implemented in this class. If the file paths resolve differently in the operating system, the mapping that the *ACADatumOSFilePathResolver* performs could result in an incorrect resource being checked for access. In the worst case, this could allow an adversary to access a file he would not normally have access to.
	Related external security notes:
	(1) *ACADatumOSFilePathResolver* is intended to be used on A. Datum Operating System 1.0 only. Using it on other platforms is not supported and could cause errors.
	(4) Users who implement the *IACPathResolver* interface should be sure to use the same parsing and normalization as the underlying system that stores the resource. This will prevent inconsistencies between path resolution in the resolver and the underlying system that could result in access checks being done on one resource in the Access Control API and another resource being opened by the underlying system.
Investigation notes	None
Entry points	(8.2) *ACADatumOSFilePathResolver*
Assets	(9.5) Accuracy of the normalized resource path
	(9.1) Read access to resources
	(9.2) Write access to resources
Threat tree	None

Table C-13   **Threat: Spoofing Another User**

ID	4
Name	Adversary spoofs user to gain another user's access rights
Description	A malicious user might try to impersonate another user to gain that user's access rights.
STRIDE classification	Spoofing
Mitigated?	Yes
Known mitigation	The application using the API must supply the correct username in the call to *ACCheck.CheckAccess*. Usernames in the Access Control API are compared by using a literal string comparison and are case sensitive.
Investigation notes	None
Entry points	(5) *ACUsers*
Assets	(9.1) Read access to resources
	(9.2) Write access to resources
Threat tree	None

Table C-14   **Threat: Spoofing Group Membership**

ID	5
Name	Adversary spoofs group membership to gain that group's access rights
Description	A malicious user might try to spoof group membership to gain the access rights of the group.
STRIDE classification	Spoofing
Mitigated?	Yes
Known mitigation	The application using the Access Control API must configure and maintain group membership. This is done directly via the API and is not persisted to disk or any other store that could be tampered with by the adversary.
Investigation notes	None
Entry points	(3) *ACGroups*
Assets	(9.3) Group membership
	(9.1) Read access to resources
	(9.2) Write access to resources
Threat tree	None

Table C-15 Threat: Causing a Denial of Service by Providing a Complex Pathname

ID	6
Name	Adversary causes denial of service by providing a complicated pathname
Description	An attacker might use a resource path that requires greater-than-average processing or memory resources to parse, causing a denial of service to other users.
STRIDE classification	Denial of service
Mitigated?	Yes
Known mitigation	See investigation notes.
Investigation notes	A code review and performance test of the supplied implementation of the *IACPathResolver* (*ACADatumOSFilePathResolver*) did not find any compute-intensive operations.
	A code review and test of the *ACResources.Get* API showed that the implementation used a recursive function call each time a path separator character was encountered. If a long enough path comprising path separator characters is supplied, the application could run out of memory on the stack, causing a fault. Because the fault is not handled, it crashes the application.
Entry points	(8) *IACPathResolver*
	(1.3) *Get*
Assets	(8.1) Availability
Threat tree	None

Table C-16 Threat: Denial of Service Attack

ID	7
Name	Adversary causes denial of service by repeatedly requesting implicitly generated nodes
Description	Because implicitly generated nodes are not persisted, an attacker could try repeatedly requesting access to one of these nodes. This could result in a denial of service if the implicitly generated nodes are not created efficiently.
STRIDE classification	Denial of service
Mitigated?	Yes
Known mitigation	The Access Control API test team has tests that cover this scenario. Performance in such cases does not degrade significantly.
Investigation notes	None
Entry points	(1) *ACResources*
Assets	(8.1) Availability
Threat tree	None

Table C-17   Threat: Determining if a Path Exists

ID	8
Name	Adversary determines whether a specified path exists
Description	The adversary might want to determine whether a specific path that he should not have access to exists. This can include finding out whether the path exists in the resource tree or in the underlying system.
STRIDE classification	Information disclosure
Mitigated?	Partially
Known mitigation	This is partially mitigated because the Access Control API never interacts with the underlying system that stores the resources.
Investigation notes	None
Entry points	(1) *ACResources*
Assets	(9.6) Path discovery
Threat tree	

Table C-18   Threat: Access Without Auditing

ID	9
Name	Adversary accesses a resource without being logged or audited
Description	An adversary who can attempt to access a resource without being logged or audited could perform an attack without the administrator knowing or being able to take action against the attack.

Table C-18 Threat: Access Without Auditing

STRIDE classification	Repudiation
Mitigated?	No
Known mitigation	None
Investigation notes	None
Entry points	(7) *ACCheck*
Assets	(9.7) Audit data
Threat tree	None

Table C-19 Threat: Bypassing a Deny Access Control Entry

ID	10
Name	Adversary with a Deny gains access to a resource
Description	Denies have precedence over Grants. In complex configurations of Grants and Denies, the adversary should not be able to take advantage of a logic error granting her access when she should be denied.
STRIDE classification	Elevation of privilege
Mitigated?	No
Known mitigation	None
Investigation notes	The following check is performed for the read/write access on the *DenyFlags:*

```
boolean DenyResult = (AccessFlags & DeniedFlags);
```

This results in the following table of possibilities:

```
AccessFlags = 0, DeniedFlags = 0, Result = false
AccessFlags = 1, DeniedFlags = 0, Result = false
AccessFlags = 2, DeniedFlags = 0, Result = false
AccessFlags = 3, DeniedFlags = 0, Result = false

AccessFlags = 0, DeniedFlags = 1, Result = false
AccessFlags = 1, DeniedFlags = 1, Result = true
AccessFlags = 2, DeniedFlags = 1, Result = false
AccessFlags = 3, DeniedFlags = 1, Result = true

AccessFlags = 0, DeniedFlags = 2, Result = false
AccessFlags = 1, DeniedFlags = 2, Result = false
AccessFlags = 2, DeniedFlags = 2, Result = true
AccessFlags = 3, DeniedFlags = 2, Result = true

AccessFlags = 0, DeniedFlags = 3, Result = false
AccessFlags = 1, DeniedFlags = 3, Result = true
AccessFlags = 2, DeniedFlags = 3, Result = true
AccessFlags = 3, DeniedFlags = 3, Result = true
```

This table shows that the flag comparison is correct. However, the way that the user/group Deny is calculated is incorrect. (See the corresponding DFD for *ACCheck.CheckAccess* and the threat tree in this table.)

Table C-19   **Threat: Bypassing a Deny Access Control Entry**

Entry points	(7) *ACCheck*
Assets	(9.1) Read access to resources
	(9.2) Write access to resources
Threat tree	

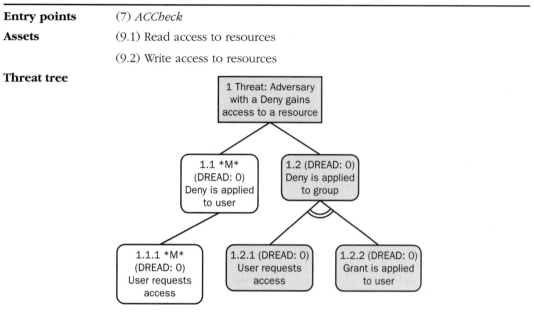

Table C-20   **Threat: Denial of Service by Malicious Input**

ID	11
Name	Adversary causes denial of service by forcing a null pointer dereference
Description	A user might try requesting nonexistent resources or other items to cause a null dereference, crashing the application.
STRIDE classification	Denial of service
Mitigated?	Yes
Known mitigation	A code review for this type of error was performed, and no problems were found.
Investigation notes	A. Datum's standard code review sessions look for null-dereference errors. All code in the Access Control API was reviewed to this standard, and no errors were found.
Entry points	(1) *ACResources*
Assets	(8.1) Availability
Threat tree	None

Vulnerabilities

The known vulnerabilities to the Access Control API system are listed in a series of tables in this section—one table for each vulnerability. Each table includes the risk associated with not fixing the vulnerability so that the threat modeling team can choose mitigation strategies appropriately.

Table C-21   Vulnerability: Buffer Overflow in Path Processing

ID	1
Name	Null-character overflow in path buffer allocation
Description	When the buffer to copy the supplied path is calculated, it does not include the terminating (null) character. This results in a one-character overflow when the path is copied (because the null character is copied to the destination buffer).
STRIDE classification	Elevation of privilege
DREAD rating	10
Corresponding threat	2: Adversary causes a buffer or integer overflow by providing a path of a overly long length
Bug	6654

Table C-22   Vulnerability: Integer Overflow in Path Processing

ID	2
Name	Integer overflow in path length computation for paths greater than 65,535 characters
Description	The path length is calculated by using an unsigned short integer (16 bits). This means that a path longer than 64 k will cause integer rollover so that the calculated length will actually be
	ActualLength MOD 65536
	Thus, for an actual length of 65,537 characters, only 1 character will be allocated. When the path is copied, arbitrary memory beyond the one-character allocation will be overwritten with the input path.
STRIDE classification	Elevation of privilege
DREAD rating	10
Corresponding threat	2: Adversary causes a buffer or integer overflow by providing an overly long path
Bug	6656

Table C-23   Vulnerability: Denial of Service Through Path Processing

ID	3
Name	Long path of path separator characters supplied to *ACResources.Get* can cause the application to crash
Description	The *ACResources.Get* API uses a recursive function call each time a path separator character is encountered. If a long enough path comprising path separator characters is supplied, the application could run out of memory on the stack, causing a fault. Because the fault is not handled, it crashes the application. This recursive algorithm should be removed.
	Usage information culled from A. Datum's customer activity shows that most use limits path lengths, typically to less than 4096 characters. This number is typically less than that required to run out of space for stack frames; therefore, the affected number of users is low.
STRIDE classification	Denial of service
DREAD rating	9
Corresponding threat	6: Adversary causes denial of service by providing complicated pathname
Bug	6657

Table C-24   Vulnerability: Determining if a Path Exists

ID	4
Name	Requesting no access flags for a resource that exists when Explicit mode is set
Description	If no access flags are set when access is requested for a resource that exists and Explicit mode is set, the API will always return true. If the resource does not exist, it will return an error code indicating that the resource was not found. This behavior should be changed so that it does not allow an adversary to determine whether a path exists in the resource tree.
STRIDE classification	Information disclosure
DREAD rating	4.8
Corresponding threat	8: Adversary discovers whether a specified path exists
Bug	6670

Table C-25   Vulnerability: No Auditing on Requests

ID	5
Name	No logging or auditing occurs in the Access Control API
Description	The Access Control API currently has no logging or auditing facilities. Instead, the application using the host must log data. However, it is the responsibility of the Access Control API to promote users creating secure, robust systems.
STRIDE classification	Repudiation
DREAD rating	5
Corresponding threat	9: Adversary accesses a resource without being logged or audited
Bug	6673

Table C-26   Vulnerability: Deny Access Control Entries Handled Incorrectly

ID	6
Name	Deny applied to a group and Grant applied to user incorrectly calculates access
Description	If a user is granted access to a resource, that access will override the check made by *ACCheck.CheckAccess* and return access granted. (See the corresponding DFD.) If that user is a member of a group that is denied access, the check for the group will never occur. Because Denies must take precedence, regardless of whether they are applied to a user or to a group, this results in an exploitable condition.
STRIDE classification	Elevation of privilege
DREAD rating	7.2
Corresponding threat	10: Adversary with a Deny gains access to a resource previously inaccessible to him
Bug	6679

Index

I

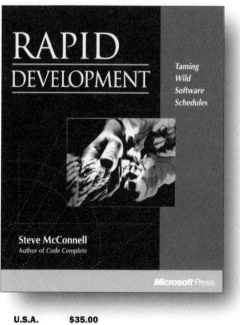

About the Authors

Frank Swiderski currently works for Microsoft as a software security engineer and is responsible for helping Microsoft product teams evaluate the impact of threats to their product or component. He has specialized in application security for several years, including serving as a security architect for @stake, a leading digital security consulting firm.

Window Snyder is a program manager for Microsoft on the Secure Windows Initiative Team. Prior to joining Microsoft, Window was director of security architecture for @stake, a security consulting firm. She has spent eight years in the security industry as a consultant and as a software engineer.

What do you think of this book?
We want to hear from you!

Do you have a few minutes to participate in a brief online survey? Microsoft is interested in hearing your feedback about this publication so that we can continually improve our books and learning resources for you.

To participate in our survey, please visit:

www.microsoft.com/learning/booksurvey

And enter this book's ISBN, 0-7356-1991-3. As a thank-you to survey participants in the United States and Canada, each month we'll randomly select five respondents to win one of five $100 gift certificates from a leading online merchant.* At the conclusion of the survey, you can enter the drawing by providing your e-mail address, which will be used for prize notification *only*.

Thanks in advance for your input. Your opinion counts!

Sincerely,

Microsoft® Learning

Learn More. Go Further.

To see special offers on Microsoft Learning products for developers, IT professionals, and home and office users, visit: *www.microsoft.com/learning/booksurvey*